Router Projects

Router Projects

FOR THE

Woodworker

STOBART DAVIES LTD
HERTFORD

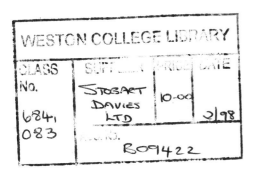
British Library Cataloguing in Publication Data

Router projects for woodworkers.
  1. Routers (Tools)
  621.9'3   TT203.5

  ISBN 0–85442–038–X

Published 1988, reprinted 1996 by
Stobart Davies Ltd, Priory House, 2 Priory Street, Hertford SG14 1RN

Typeset in Palatino by Photo·graphics, Honiton, Devon
Printed in Great Britain by BPC Wheatons Ltd, Exeter, Devon.

Contents

Acknowledgments and Introduction

The publishers would like to extend their thanks to all those contributors and associates who together have made this book possible.

In particular to John Costello of Elu who provided the text and illustrations for the opening chapter on the plunging router; to Betty Norbury for the many hours of initial research work; to Edward Addison for his editorial skills; and collectively to the talented authors who provided the designs.

In a book written by twenty different people, the reader enjoys a rich variety of styles and presentation. Some will be straight to the point with a no-nonsense approach, others more chatty or discursive. Similarly, when dealing with the conversion of metric to imperial measure (and vice versa), variations will be evident. One writer for example may convert $\frac{1}{2}$ inch to 12mm, another may convert to 13mm. When dealing with *precise* sizes the conversion of fractions and decimals becomes even more critical, therefore it is important that the reader is aware of the small variations which may occur during the translation from metric to imperial or from imperial to metric measure.

The above comments apply also to router cutter sizes. The editorial judgement was to round up or down the conversion factor: a $\frac{1}{4}$ inch and a $\frac{1}{2}$ inch cutter have been designated 6mm ($\frac{1}{4}''$) and 12mm ($\frac{1}{2}''$) when in reality they measure 6.35mm and 12.7mm respectively. The reader is advised therefore to personally ensure that the sizes of replacement parts and accessories fit his or her own router and its chuck size.

For us, this has proved a most pleasurable book to produce, not least because of the craftsmen and craftswomen with whom we have worked. We trust that it gives you, the reader, equal satisfaction and we very much hope that you enjoy making some, or all, of the twenty projects described. We shall be glad to hear our readers' views and to see photographs of their finished work.

BRIAN J. DAVIES
Publisher
Stobart Davies Ltd

Introducing

the

Plunging Router

and its

Accessories

Free-hand drawing with the router
(MOF96E)

Introducing the Plunging Router and its Accessories

THE hand-held router has now been in existence for over forty years. In the early years, designs were heavy, unwieldy and mostly of the fixed-base type. Then they were used almost exclusively by professional craftsmen.

More recently, however, with the development of the Plunging Router, and its resulting greatly increased safety, versatility and convenience, the demand for these machines has grown dramatically, both among a very much wider cross section of professional users as well as increasingly ambitious home-woodworking enthusiasts.

Whether the reader already owns a plunging router or is looking to purchase one in the near future, it is hoped that the following notes will prove a useful reference enabling the techniques required in making the projects featured later to be mastered with ease and safety. The project contributors are mainly professional craftsmen, using the router continuously in earning their living. The techniques involved are second nature to such operators since, after all, 'practice makes perfect'. The first thing for the novice router user to note, however, is that no great skill is needed to use one, in contrast, say, with that required when using non-powered hand tools to perform the same functions.

All that is needed to use a portable router successfully is a small amount of dexterity, which any keen amateur will possess. For someone using a router for the first time, it is often a revelation to see how easily and effortlessly work can be carried out and also how many different tasks for which the router proves to be the ideal tool.

Having said that no particular skill is needed to use one, obviously an experienced router operator will clearly be able to demonstrate the benefits that only time and extensive practice can bring.

One essential requirement, as with all portable power tools, is common-sense. The user must always be safety-conscious and appreciate that reckless operation of any portable power tool is dangerous and could result in serious injury. It is recommended that these 'Safety First' notes are read and inwardly digested, along with the manufacturers' operating instructions supplied with the machine, before any work is done.

Basic safety measures:

Take account of local conditions

Never expose electrical tools to rain, and never use them in humid or wet conditions.

Make sure you have adequate lighting.

Never use electrical tools in the vicinity of flammable liquids or gases.

Protect yourself against electric shock

Avoid touching earthed objects (e.g. pipes, radiators, ovens, refrigerators) when you are using the machine.

Keep children away

Never let other people touch the machine or cable, and keep them away from your workplace.

Keep your machine in a safe place

When not in use, power tools should be kept in a dry, lockable place out of the reach of children.

Never overload the machine

You will be able to work with greater care and comfort within the specified capacity of the machine.

Use the correct tools

Never use weak tools or accessories for heavy jobs.

Do not work with unsuitable tools.

Wear suitable clothing

Never wear loose clothing or jewellery which could be caught in moving parts of the machine.

When working outdoors, gloves and non-slip shoes are recommended.

If you have long hair, wear a hair net or tie it back.

Use protective equipment

Wear goggles and use a breathing mask in dusty conditions.

Do not use the cable for other purposes

Do not carry the machine by the cable.

Do not pull out the plug by the cable.

Protect the cable from heat, oil and sharp edges.

Support the workpiece firmly

Use a clamping device to hold the workpiece firmly in place. It will be held more firmly than by hand, and both hands will be free for operating the machine.

Maintain correct posture

Avoid abnormal stances when working.

Make sure you are standing securely and keep your balance.

Take care of your tools

Always keep your cutters sharp and clean; you will be able to work better and more safely.

Follow the instructions for maintenance and changing cutters.

Check the cable regularly and have it replaced by an authorized expert if it is damaged.

Check extension cables regularly. If they are damaged they must be replaced.

Keep handles dry and free of grease and oil.

Remove the power plug

Before maintenance work, during tool changes and when the machine is not in use, ensure that the power plug is removed from the socket.

Check

Before switching on the machine check that all keys and adjusting tools have been removed.

Avoid unintentional starting

Never carry electrical tools with your finger on the switch when they are connected to the power supply.

Make sure that the switch is in the OFF position before connecting to the mains.

Extension cables outdoors

When working outdoors, only use suitable and correspondingly labelled extension cables.

Always concentrate

Always concentrate on what you are doing. Proceed carefully. Never use the machine when you cannot concentrate.

Check the machine for damage

Carefully check the protection devices and visible parts of your machine for correct operation and function.

Also check that the moving parts operate freely, that there are no breakages, that all other parts are correctly installed and that all factors affecting the operation of the machine are in order.

Damaged protection devices and components must be repaired or replaced by an authorized service workshop.

Damaged switches must also be replaced at an authorized service workshop.

Never use electrical tools with defective switches.

Choosing a Router

Which router model is the most appropriate to use will depend on several factors, including the level of working intensity, the nature of the work involved (i.e. is it a delicate, intricate project or one simply requiring removal of a lot of material?), the size of the cutters to be used, what range of accessories is available for use with it, and inevitably the amount of money available.

Clearly, if only for occasional use then, a low-cost machine sold in the High Street will be all that is required, but beware! With routers, perhaps more than with many other products, you 'get what you pay for'! If low-price is your primary selection criterion, then you cannot expect the same operating life, reliability or setting precision which you can obtain with the more expensive machines designed for professional use.

Note also that professional woodworkers use low-weight machines for some tasks, where a heavier, high-powered router would be completely inappropriate and make the job more difficult.

Elu offers the widest range of professional routers and routing accessories available so the writer unashamedly outlines which Elu model is most appropriate to differing applications.

MOF96E

This 750 watt machine is designed for use with 6 mm ($\frac{1}{4}$″) shanked cutters and despite its power, weighs only 2.8 kg (6.16 lbs). It is, therefore, ideal for intricate work, whether involving freehand or edge moulding etc. and any other jobs using cutters with a working diameter of up to 32 mm ($1\frac{1}{4}$″). The 'E' suffix on this model (which is the one featured in the photo below),

Sectional and working views of MOF96E

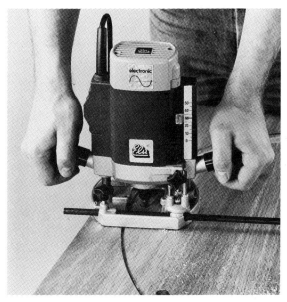

denotes full-wave electronic control, offering many practical advantages, including:

Soft start, i.e. no sudden jerk when the machine is switched on.

Speed variable between 8,000–24,000 rpm, enabling the right speed to be selected to suit the cutter diameter for efficiency, increased safety and longer cutting life.

Selected speed maintained under load, meaning the same clean, accurate results in all grades of timber, plastics and even aluminium.

Ability to set slower speeds, especially on intricate, free-hand work, reduces the risk of scorching timber.

If you do not have a need for such a level of sophistication then the single speed 600 watt version (MOF96) is available at lower cost.

MOF177E

This machine is at the other end of the scale, having 1850 watts, 65 mm ($2\frac{1}{2}''$) plunge depth (MOF96/96E = 50 mm (2″)) and is designed for use with the larger 12 mm ($\frac{1}{2}''$) cutters, although collets (the 'chuck' which grips the cutter in the machine) are also available to take 6 mm ($\frac{1}{4}''$) and the less commonly used 10 mm ($\frac{3}{8}''$) shank cutters — as well as a variety of sizes in between.

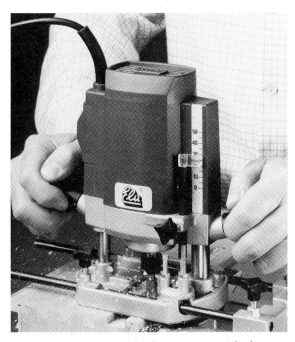

MOF96 using standard equipment side fence

The MOF177E, like the MOF96E, also has electronic control with the same benefits as above with a top speed of 20,000 rpm.

Clearly, the MOF177E is a heavy-duty machine, although its weight of 5.1 kg (11.3 lbs) still makes it easy to use on a continuing basis without causing excessive fatigue. Large

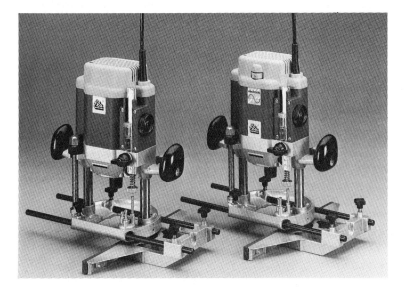

MOF177 (Left)
MOF177E (Right)

capacity cutting, trenching, rebating and shaping work with cutters up to 40 mm ($1\frac{1}{2}''$) in diameter are the jobs appropriate here, although it is not that unusual for some home woodworkers to buy this model also.

Again a single speed version, the MOF177, with 1600 watts is also available.

MOF131

Between these two extremes the MOF131 is a mid-range, single speed model with 1300 watts, which is designed for the operator using 6 mm ($\frac{1}{4}''$) shank cutters with particular intensity and also sometimes needing to mount 12 mm ($\frac{1}{2}''$) or 10 mm ($\frac{3}{8}''$) cutters for occasional work.

Elu also have other router models in their range for specialist applications and further information is available direct from the maker whose address appears at the end of this introductory section.

What to look for in a Router

That's fine, you might say, but how do I make an objective judgment between different makes of routers? Well, in the view of the writer, the following features are what you should look for in a router:

Operator Comfort: It will be safer to use and easier to be accurate, if it is well balanced and the handles are comfortable to hold and the switch easy to operate — so don't buy one before you've tried holding it.

Good Visibility: Obviously a good view of the cutting position again ensures safety and accuracy.

Collet Quality: An easy-action, good quality collet chuck to retain the cutters accurately and securely on the machine is essential.

Plunge Smoothness: The plunge action must be smooth and there should be no rocking movement of the motor housing on the columns.

Depth Setting: It must be possible to set the plunge depth easily against a clearly legible scale, with a 3-position depth stop for plunging to progressive depths and the plunge lock should be both easy to operate and positive.

Accessories: A full comprehensive range of accessories should be available to enable you to make maximum use of the router for those more advanced projects.

Recommendations for correct choice of speed (MOF96E/MOF177E)

The Electronic Models, MOF96E and MOF177E, feature infinitely variable speed (8–24,000 and 8–20,000 rpm respectively). The following table is a guide as to which should be selected depending on the material, but note that wood is a living material and therefore variable in its consistency.

Speeds indicated for each stage 1–5 are approximate only. Experience with the adjust-

● Very Suitable O Suitable ○ Can be used	**ELECTRONIC CONTROL SETTING**				
Setting	1	2	3	4	5
Approx. Speed (R.P.M.): MOF96E	8,000	10,500	16,000	21,000	24,000
MOF177E	8,000	12,000	16,000	18,000	20,000

Material	**Cutter**	1	2	3	4	5
Hardwood e.g. Oak	Small			○	O	●
	Medium			○	●	O
	Large	O	●	○		
Softwood e.g. Pine	Small			○	O	●
	Medium		○	O	●	●
	Large	O	●	○		
Plastic-Laminated Chipboard	Small			○	O	●
	Medium			○	O	O
	Large	○	O	●	○	
Plastics	Small			○	O	●
	Medium			O	●	O
	Large	O	●	○		
Aluminium	Small		●	O	○	
	Medium	O	●	○		
	Large	●	O	○		
Cup-Shaped Cutters Softwoods, e.g. Pine Veneered Panels Plastic-coated Chipboard		○	O	●	O	●

When feeding material at a rapid rate, set the electronic control at one stage higher than indicated in the table.

able speed feature will also suggest that intermediate setting between the numbered positions on the control wheel are sometimes appropriate. Remember that these are 'full-wave' electronic machines and the speed selected is therefore maintained under load.

The motor in the MOF177E is different from that in the MOF96E and it has a different power and speed curve which explains the reason for the speed variances at stages 2, 4 and 5 but this does not affect the recommendation of stage settings between the two models.

Types of Router Cutters available

Having decided which router is most appropriate for your task, select the type of cutter required for the job in view — you can do nothing with a router until a cutter, or a 'bit' of some description, has been mounted in it.

Different diameter straight bits for channelling and rebating.

Narrow straight bits, for channelling and letter work.

Veining bit for decorative work.

'V' grooving cutter for chamfers and grooves.

Core box cutter for grooves, edge profiles and drop-leaf joints.

Rebating cutter for easy narrow rebates.

Corner round cutter for profiles and drop-leaf joints.

Roman ogee cutter for really professional decorative profiles.

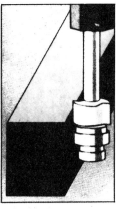

Laminate cutter for clearly finished laminates and veneers.

16

There are basically two types of cutters:

Firstly, there are the cutters without any guide — and a wide range of cutter profiles are of this type. Used for forming decorative edges, and surface cuts, these cutters are used either in conjunction with the router's parallel fence, free-hand across the face of the work with or without a template guide, or with the router in stationary mode mounted upside down in a router bench.

The second type of cutters are those with pilots, which can be either of the fixed type or have a rotating ball-bearing. Both are used at the edge of the workpiece with the pilot acting as the guide, making the parallel fence superfluous. With such cutters, obviously the amount of material which can be removed is limited to the distance between the end of the cutter and the outside face of the pilot.

Within these types, there is a choice of material from which the cutters are made — High Speed Steel (HSS) or Tungsten Carbide Tipped (TCT). HSS cutters are the best for projects in natural wood, but the much more expensive (and longer-life) TCT are really necessary for man-made board and other materials.

Some of the basic cutter types are shown here, but it would be possible to fill a whole book of this size with the range of sizes and types which are generally available. The illustrations show what might be appropriate as a 'Beginner's Kit', with more specialist types to be added as the user's experience develops.

Template Work

One of the most creative uses of a router is in conjunction with your own design of template. Most routers are supplied with one template guide and a range of other sizes are available as optional accessories. The guide allows the router to follow precisely the shape of the template for producing all kinds of decorative work, for cutting recesses, as needed for hinges, for example, and for boring accurately-positioned vertical holes for dowels etc. For repetition-cutting of irregular shapes, the template

and guide offer a speedy and efficient method of operation. The drawing shows how the guide can follow any shape within the template to duplicate that shape on the workpiece.

Template design

Having selected a template guide bush — which forms a short skirt outside the cutter under the base of the router — and decided which bit to use with it, you can design a template for the cut you want to make. Plywood or dense hardboard are ideal materials, about 10 mm ($\frac{3}{8}$″) being the best thickness. A template

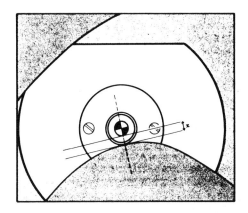

with a cutout for the router to work inside needs to be bigger than the finished cut, but where the outside edge has to be followed by the bush the template has to be smaller than the cut. In each case, the amount by which the template must be larger or smaller is the distance (X) from the outer edge of the protruding bush to the bit's cutting edge. This is most easily and accurately measured by making a trial cut in a piece of scrap wood against a straight batten and checking the width of the step produced with a steel rule.

Grooving

Grooves are widely used in woodworking. A portable router provides the fastest of all methods for cutting grooves. It produces an absolutely clean cut and the accuracy of the groove is such as to ensure a good fit with the mating tongue.

To produce a straight groove in the correct position, it is essential that the side fence is used when working on narrow workpieces.

In the case of wider workpieces attach a straight batten or steel straight-edge to the workpiece.

Grooves are used for a wide variety of purposes. The following are some examples.

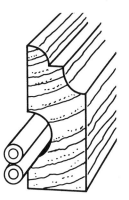

Trap to throw off rainwater on underside of door or window sill.

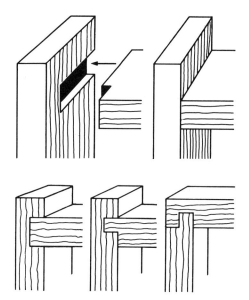

Grooves to accommodate shelves, open and stopped types.

Groove to accomodate cables in a skirting board.

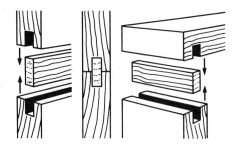

Grooves for wood joints, also square joints with a loose tongue. The width of the tongue is 3 mm ($\frac{1}{8}$") less than the combined depth of the two grooves.

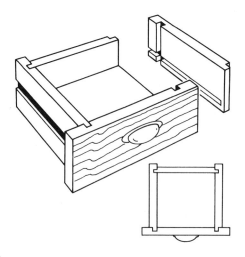

Various grooves for a variety of purposes, for example on a drawer.

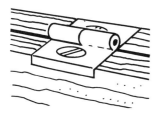

Housings for hinges are in a sense also grooves. During machining the two boards are clamped together so that their edges are flush.

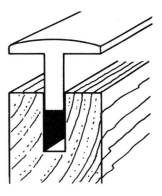

This simple groove is used to house a plastic edge strip.

Rebating

Like grooving, rebating is a very common task when working wood. The machine set-up and the procedure is the same as for grooving. The same work can also be performed with the machine set up as a portable router with a right-angle base (also in stationary form) or as a spindle moulder.

Rebates are used for a wide variety of purposes, and are required in many wood structures, as shown in the following illustrations.

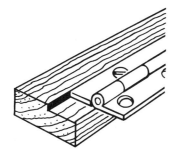

For housing a piano hinge.

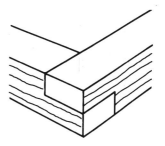

A half lap corner joint.

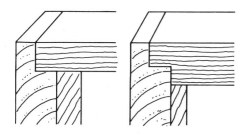

The rebate as a joint element. On left a recessed rear panel. On right a corner joint.

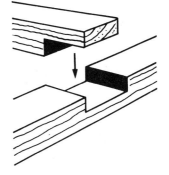

A half lap joint employing a groove of appropriate width.

A half lap butt joint.

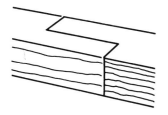

A half lap joint.

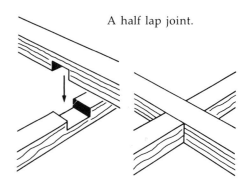

Mitre Cutting

Every amateur woodworker is bound at some time or other to have found that a sawn mitre does not fit properly. With a routed mitre, on the other hand, it is possible to be absolutely sure that the edge will have a clean finish and that the mitre will fit properly.

A mitre such as this

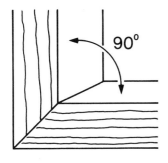

is produced as follows using the router.

Use a 'V' chamfering cutter.

Clamp a surplus board (to protect the bench) and the workpiece onto the bench. Make sure that all three edges — of the bench, the board, and the workpieces — are flush one above the other. Also make sure that these edges are at right-angles to the surface of the bench or workpiece. This can be checked most accurately with the aid of a square.

Now line the machine up, using the side fence and the depth of cut adjustment, so that the guide pin on the chamfering cutter bears against the edge of the board protecting the bench. It is also important for the top

face of this board to line up accurately with the 'corner' between the guide pin and the flute on the cutter. When the machine is properly set up, make the cut by passing the machine along the workpiece.

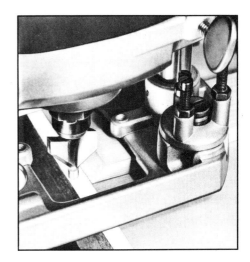

Mitres can be cut on material having a thickness of up to 16 mm ($\frac{5}{8}''$) by this method. It is advisable to perform the cut in two stages.

Making Mouldings

Moulded edges can take a wide variety of shapes and will greatly improve the appearance of a workpiece, giving it an individual character.

A wide variety of cutters are suitable for this purpose. If cutters with straight flutes are unsuitable, use cutters producing concave or convex curves.

In many cases the combined use of several different cutters on the same workpiece, or even on the same edge, will produce interesting shapes.

The following illustrations show a number of examples of simple and compound mouldings.

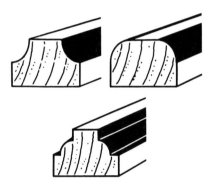

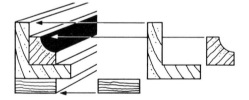

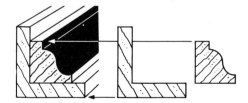

Trimming Edges

The task here is not to mould the edge to a specific shape, but rather to remove the material that projects beyond a given edge. This occurs, for example, if a solid wood strip is fitted round the edge of a veneered panel, and the two surfaces are not exactly flush so that the edge strip projects beyond the panel.

A more frequent case however, is that in which the projecting material is a plastic laminate. These hard, but very brittle materials are difficult to trim with normal tools, but not with a router. Accurate trimming of plastic laminate panels is of special importance for those who apply such panels to their workpiece themselves. When the panel is applied to the workpiece it must be placed so that it projects about 3 mm ($\frac{1}{8}''$) beyond the edge of the workpiece.

It is also important to see that the edge of the workpiece itself is clean and level without any traces of glue — since the cutter or machine uses this edge as a guide. Select the appropriate cutter depending on whether the projecting portion is to be trimmed off flush with the edge of the workpiece or is to be chamfered.

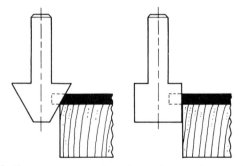

If the excess material projects above the surface the cutter can be used as follows:

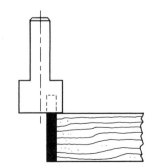

If the excess material projects from both the top and bottom surfaces of the panel, and you are using an Elu router or another with a similar parallel fence arrangement, take the plastic angle strip off the fence of the router reverse it and screw it on again with the leg of the angle facing away from the fence.

The leg of the angle will then bear against the edge of the workpiece between the projecting edges of the top and bottom sheets. This then enables the fence to guide the machine properly, and both projecting surfaces can be trimmed off simultaneously.

Edge trimming can be performed equally with all four possible arrangements of the machine. But one or other of the arrangements will prove the most successful for one or other type of work.

It is important to adjust the cutter accurately.

Once again it is advisable to make a trial cut first.

Drilling Dowel Holes

Joints in woodwork that use dowels are much simpler to produce than dovetail joints, and despite this are very strong and rigid.

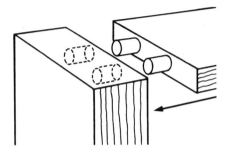

Difficulties are often encountered in centring the dowel holes precisely, and any inaccuracies here can ruin the job. Using the router and guide bush with a diameter of 17 mm ($\frac{5}{8}''$) and a home-made template, that has 17 mm ($\frac{5}{8}''$) diameter holes and is fitted with an accurately-positioned batten for use as a fence or stop, accurate drilling of the dowel holes is no

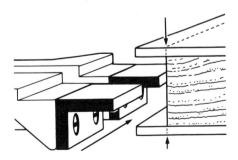

problem, since the guide bush in conjunction with the template enables the hole to be accurately centred.

Cutting Mortises for Tenon Joints

A slot in which a tenon fits accurately will produce another very rigid joint in wood.

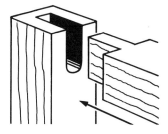

The method of producing the tenon is basically the same as for rebating. The work can be performed with the machine used as a portable router, but preferably arranged as a router with a right-angle base, especially if set up for stationary use, or arranged as a spindle moulder. Some explanation of the method of cutting the mortise is necessary:

The mortise can be cut right through, in which case the tenon will be visible.

A mortise and tenon joint in which the mortise is not cut right through, so that the tenon cannot be seen from the outside, is

equally strong and rigid. In this case the mortise should be cut to a depth about 5 mm ($\frac{3}{16}$") more than the length of the tenon.

Pick a straight cutter that has the correct cutter head diameter, e.g. the same as the width of the mortise. If the diameter of the cutter is less than the width of the mortise the cut will have to be made in stages.

Mark the start and finish of the mortise, ie. its length.

Cut the mortise to the required depth at one end, and then move the router along to the other end.

If the depth of the mortise is more than can be cut in a single pass, repeat until the required depth is achieved. This completes the mortise.

Mortises can be cut with the router, either using the machine as a portable router with a fence, without a template, or alternatively a template can be used in which case the fence will not be required.

When mortising or rebating narrow edges a second parallel fence may be desirable for improved stability and accuracy.

Optional attachments and accessories to further extend the versatility, speed and accuracy of the router

Most routers available have a parallel or side fence included as standard equipment, as well as at least one size of collet and template guide, plus, of course, the necessary spanners and instruction leaflet.

Before using the router, you have to buy the necessary cutter(s) to do the job you have in mind. However, apart from cutters, some manufacturers, and Elu in particular, offer a wide range of other optional extras which really do extend the usefulness of these most versatile power tools. The more popular items from this range are detailed below. The more specialised accessories are excluded leaving the reader to obtain the necessary information direct from the manufacturers themselves.

Miniature spindle moulding kit

Sometimes simply referred to as 'the accessory kit' because of its myriad uses, the E40900 is designed for use with the Elu MOF96/96E series, although some other router manufacturers have coincidentally designed their machines to be compatible with it also. In essence, this kit turns the portable router into a miniature spindle moulder for either vertical or horizontal stationary use, as shown in the photographs. The large surface right angle base also makes the unit very easy to guide accurately for edge-moulding jobs.

The kit also includes a trammel bar, which enables curved and circular work to be done accurately on the router in portable mode, as well as a fine height adjuster providing benefits for both stationary and portable working.

ELU MOF96/96E in action with E40900 miniature spindle-moulding unit

Above: Moulding produced to your own unique design (E40500 unit, plus E40512 secondary pressure guard and E40913 pressure block, with MOF36E attached).

Left: Accurate guidance and uniform edge moulding assured by large surface right-angle base (supplied in Accessory Kit E40900).

24

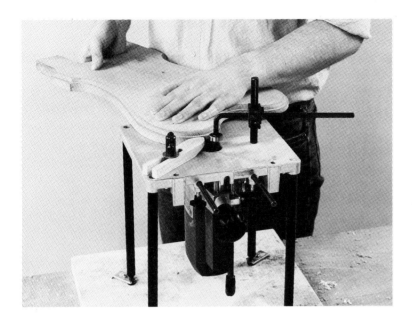

Spindle moulder base with copying roller provides for easy profiling of curved edges.

Right-angle base held stationary and router used horizontally for moulding rebates.

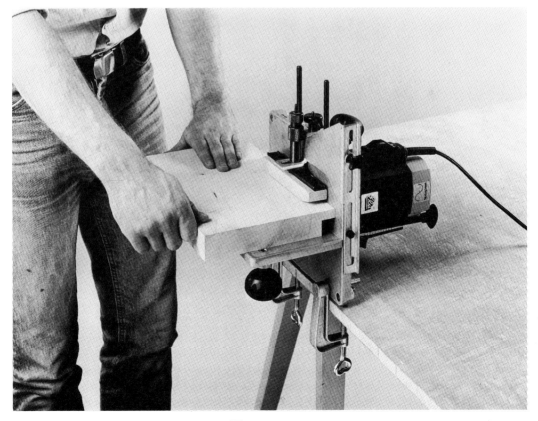

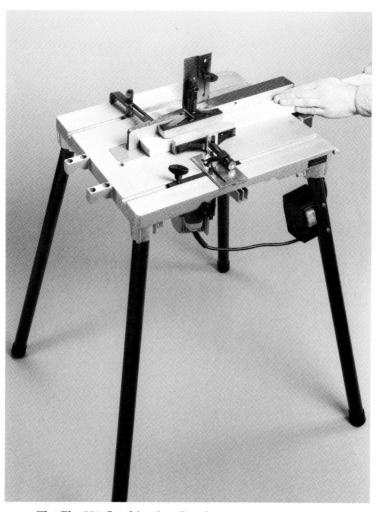

The Elu 551 Combination Bench converts your portable
router into an effective spindle moulder. Shown here
also with an optional side pressure guard E35126, fence
clamp E35123 and fine adjuster E40266.
Note: *Elu 551 is suitable for use with all Elu Plunging
Routers.*

Combination Bench

The Elu 551 Combination Bench is intended
for operators wanting to use the larger Elu
MOF131/177/177E Routers for spindle-moulding, but it will also take the smaller MOF96/
96E machines. Its large 395 × 485 mm
($15\frac{1}{2}'' \times 19''$) table surface area enables much
bigger material to be worked than the miniature
kit will allow.

It has the added advantage of being adaptable
for use also with Elu portable circular saws.

Dovetailing Attachment

Designed for use with the Elu MOF96/96E
series of Routers, this attachment can also be
used with the larger Elu Routers and other
makes if the appropriate sub-base is fitted to
the router.

The addition of a fine height adjuster makes
for easier setting, otherwise everything is provided, including the 6 mm ($\frac{1}{4}''$) shank TCT cutter,
to produce accurate and attractive 12 mm ($\frac{1}{2}''$)
dovetails in timber 12–30 mm ($\frac{1}{2}''$–$1\frac{3}{16}''$) thick and

Professional corner joints easily made using the dovetailing attachment.

up to 300 mm (11¾") wide, which is more than adequate for most drawer-making applications.

While the above attachments are relatively high value, the following are comparatively 'pocket-money' items, but nonetheless of considerable practical benefit to the enthusiast.

Template Guide Set

The standard equipment template guide will be adequate for a lot of template work, but there are many jobs where both larger and smaller diameter guide bushes are more appropriate. Elu offer a set of 12 sizes, from 10–32 mm (⅜"–1¼") in diameter, which fit directly onto the base of the MOF96/96E and also onto other models via the circular sub-base accessory.

Additional side fence and fine adjusters

For precision shaping and grooving, slotting or rebating operations, the addition of a second parallel fence and fine height and side-fence adjusters make the task a lot easier.

Template Work. A full set of 12 guide bushes 10–32 mm ($\frac{3}{8}''$–$1\frac{1}{4}''$) diameter E44173 is available to suit a range of cutter sizes and template requirements. Minimum template thickness is 6.4 mm ($\frac{1}{4}''$).

Accurate recessing using a home-made template and the standard equipment template guide, 17 mm ø ($\frac{11}{16}''$).

Accurate grooving, mortising or rebating using an extra side fence and fine adjusters.

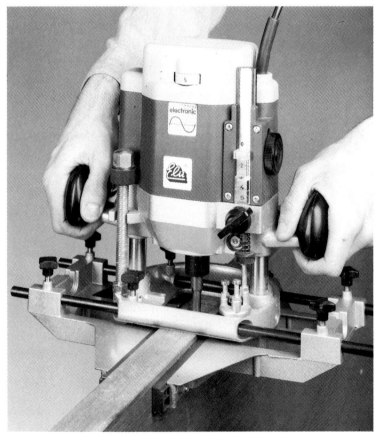

Precision grooving with the optional tracking kit.

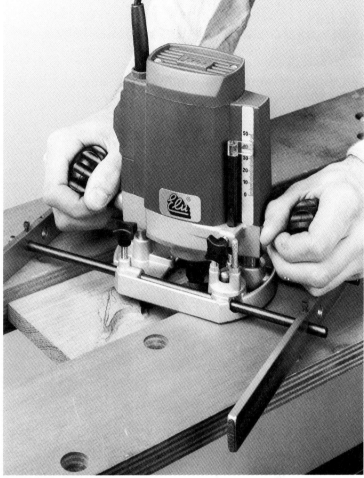

Relief Carving with Ski Attachment E44187.

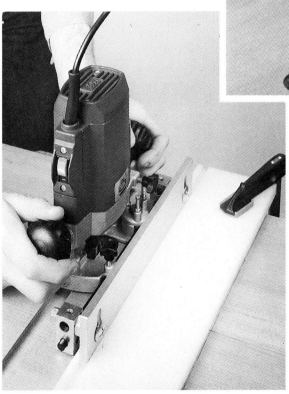

Tracking Kit

When the project requires straight line work across the face of the material, beyond the reach of the normal side fence, it is necessary to clamp a batten across it against which the base of the router can be guided. That, however, requires the operator to hold the machine firmly against the batten for the complete pass.

The alternative is to use a Tracking Kit, which consists of a tough nylon guide, with a channel cut into it, in which a steel follower attached to the router's fence rod runs along giving smooth and easy movement in a perfectly straight line.

'Ski' attachment

Fielded treatment of a sign or panel will give that individual, creative touch to any project. The ski-bars fit the fence rods and allow the extra support necessary as the router 'straddles' the work. In addition to relief carving, this attachment can also prove useful for rebating window bars, putty removal etc.

Dust Control Kit

To conclude this less-than-exhaustive enumeration of the optional attachments available for a plunging router, the question of dust control must be last but by no means the least important topic.

Due to the amount of material removed in the routing process, dust can be a problem and the operator is well advised to wear dust protection for the eyes, nose and mouth.

Even without a justifiable concern for health and safety in the face of the often noxious substances concealed in hardwood, man-made boards, MDF etc, it is also much more efficient to connect direct to an industrial vacuum cleaner to control waste disposal.

Elimination of the dust problem also greatly improves operator visibility and cutting efficiency.

More details about Elu Routers and their optional attachments and accessories may be obtained from: Elu Power Tools, Westpoint, The Grove, Slough, Berkshire, SL1 1QQ, England.

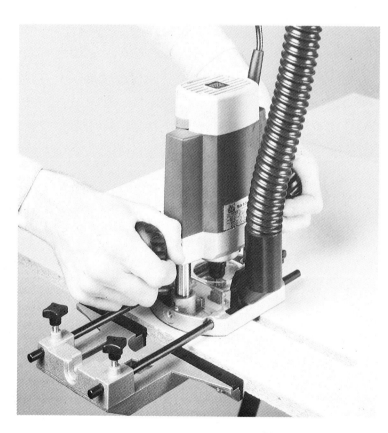

MOF96E with Dust Collection Accessory.

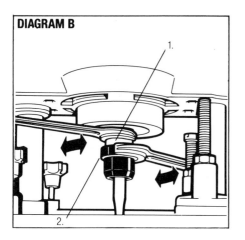

DIAGRAM B

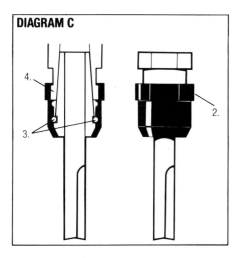

DIAGRAM C

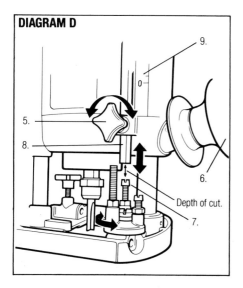

DIAGRAM D

The following notes apply to most makes of plunging router:

Fitting a Cutter (Diagram B)

Always switch off at the mains before changing cutters.

IMPORTANT NOTE:

Do not tighten the collet nut if:

a) there is no cutter in the collet
b) the cutter does not have precisely the right shank diameter for the collet. Irreparable damage to the collet will result in both cases.

1. Hold the motor spindle with the smaller spanner applied to the flats (1).
2. Ensuring that the collet chuck threads are free from dust and wood particles, insert the cutter into the collet.
3. With the larger spanner applied to the collet nut (2) tighten it up. *Do not use excessive force, a few turns will usually suffice.*
4. When removing the cutter, one turn of the collet nut (2) will release the collet, a further turn being needed to release the cutter.

Changing a Collet (Diagram C)

Always switch off at the mains before changing collets

1. Remove the collet assembly from the motor spindle. The collet is attached to the nut by means of annular springs (3) and will come out in one piece.
2. Pull the collet (4) from the collet nut (2) (a strong tug is needed).
3. Insert the new collet into the nut and push it right home.

N.B. Ensure that the bottom face of the collet is flush with the bottom face of the collet nut.

Setting the Depth Stop (Diagram D)

1. Loosen clamp screw (5) and router lock control handle (6).
2. Push router down slowly until cutter is in contact with workpiece.
3. Tighten router lock control handle.
4. The depth of cut will be equal to the distance between the head of the bolt on the bolt

31

stop (7) and the end of the depth stop bar (8).

5. The depth of cut can be gauged by using the graduated scale (9). Alternatively, a sample fitting of the depth of cut required can be placed between the bolt stop and the depth stop bar to gauge the depth (see photo).

6. When several cuts are to be made at different depths in the material the three bolts on the bolt stop (7) are adjusted accordingly.

NOTE

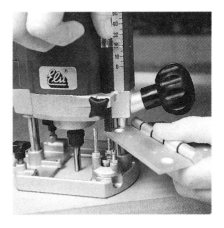

The depth of cut that can be achieved will vary according to the diameter of the cutter and the density of the material being worked. In order to achieve a clean and controlled cut, it is best to make two or more passes over the workpiece until the desired depth of cut is reached. The three stage bolt stop (7) will enable you to make a series of cuts at varying depths whilst retaining complete control. To set the right cutting depth for a particular piece of hardware, for example, a hinge, loosen the thumb screw holding the depth gauge and, with the cutter in place, press the handles gently down until the cutter just contacts the workpiece and is therefore dead level with the router base — and lock this setting with the clamping knob. Now put the hinge between the screw and the depth stop rod, lower the rod on to the hinge and clamp it. You now know that the bit can't cut any farther below the base than this very precisely gauged gap. Take the hinge away, unclamp the motor, and you're ready to make the cut as soon as the fence is set.

Feed direction

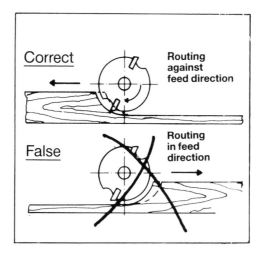

20
Projects for
Craftsmen

1. Wall-mounted Weather Board

Vic Taylor

THIS weather board was made up to accommodate a barometer, a circular thermometer and a hygrometer, and to incorporate them into a handsome accessory to hang on the wall. Obviously, your weather instruments will be of different sizes or even shapes (a "stick" thermometer instead of a round one, for instance). In Fig. 1, therefore, I have given a squared-off drawing of the design of my particular board which you may well want to adapt to your requirements.

The wood used was 19mm ($\frac{3}{4}$″) thick sapele which proved very suitable for the purpose. Fig. 2 shows how the instruments are fixed in

their holes and you can see that the depth of the drum containing the "works", combined with the length of the bolts which hold on the back-cover plates, determine the thickness of the timber to be used.

There are several ways to cut out the basic shape and Fig. 3 shows two of them. In (A) the bearings guide needs a template; and so does the guide bush in (B). I did not use either of these methods, as it seemed to me that as it was necessary to cut out the template with a jigsaw, one might as well dispense with the template and simply jigsaw the board to shape. Once the shape had been sawn, I went round

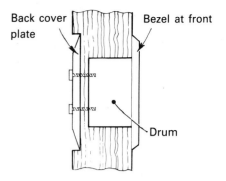

Fig. 2 The most usual way in which instruments are fitted into the board

it with a router bit which had an integral guide pin; Fig. 3 shows its profile. You, of course, can choose whatever profile you fancy provided it has a guide pin; I would recommend either the ovolo (beading) cutter or the Roman ogee, both of which are available with a guide pin.

Routing round the shape is not as simple as it sounds, and there are several points to bear in mind as follows:

(a) When you have sawn out the shape, keep the offcut. While cutting, the router has to be kept level and the best way to do this is to arrange the shape and the offcut side by side on a baseboard, leaving a space between them for the router bit to travel in. In Fig. 4 you can see the set-up; you may either fix both components to the baseboard with double-sided adhesive tape, or use cramps. If you do use double-sided tape be sure to strip it off when the work is finished by pulling it along the grain; if you attempt to strip it off across the grain you can very easily tear the wood.

(b) As the router travels round there is a tendency for the bottom of the guide pin to catch on the smallest irregularity on the surface of the baseboard; this makes a jerky movement of the router and often causes an uneven cut on the workpiece and also burn marks on the baseboard. To counter this I set the depth of cut as shown in Fig. 4 so that the thickness of the piece of paper (which you remove before routing) gives sufficient clearance.

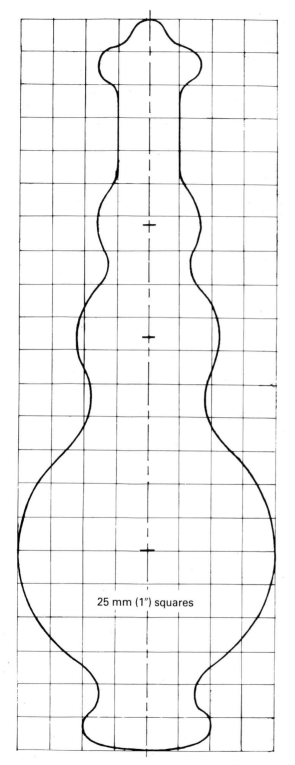

25 mm (1") squares

Fig. 1 Squared-off outline of the shape; 25 mm (1") squares

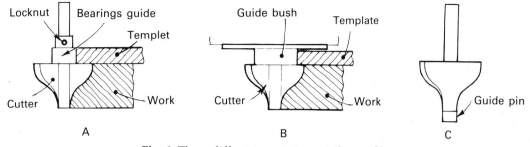

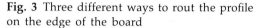

A   B   C

Fig. 3 Three different ways to rout the profile on the edge of the board

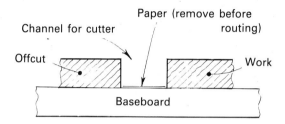

Fig. 4 Showing how the board and the offcut are positioned to form a channel for the router cutter. The cutter is plunged to touch the piece of paper, which is removed before routing – this ensures that the end of the cutter does not bind on the baseboard

(c) You are almost certain to get burn marks. The classic causes of burning are that either the cutter is blunt or, more likely, the feed speed is too slow. On straight routing you can avoid the problem by increasing the feed speed, but when routing intricate and tightly-curved shapes as in this case, the feed speed has to be slow to negotiate them.

However, there is an easy way to get rid of the marks. When you have made your first cut remove the shaped board and the offcut; stick them down again, with a piece of thin card between them and the baseboard. Keep the same setting on your router and go round the shape again; the thickness of the card will cause the router cutter to remove just a light skim and with it the burn marks.

The next job is to cut the circles for the inlays; here we have to bear in mind that the smallest circle which can be described using the standard trammel supplied with the router

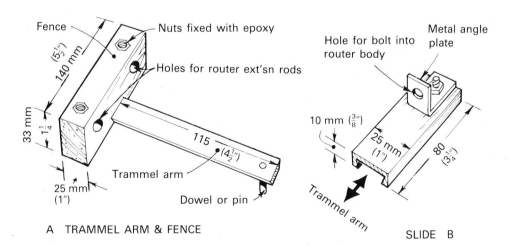

A   TRAMMEL ARM & FENCE   SLIDE   B

Fig. 5 Details of the attachment for routing small circles.

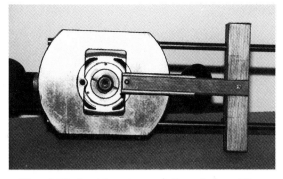

Fig. 6 Underside view of the circle-cutting attachment. When routing, a levelling piece must be attached on the opposite side of the router's sole plate

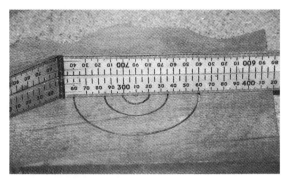

Fig. 7 Photo of three experimental circles routed with the attachment: the smallest is 20mm ($\frac{3}{4}$") diameter

is about 75mm (3") – two of the circles we need are smaller than that.

To overcome the problem, you will need to make up the accessory shown in Figs. 5 and 6. The first job is to make the slide and this comprises a piece of a close-grained timber such as beech 80mm long × 25mm wide × 10mm thick ($3\frac{1}{4}$''' × 1" × $\frac{3}{8}$") – Fig. 5B. It has a dovetail-shaped channel routed out 5mm ($\frac{3}{16}$") deep; the next task is to make the trammel arm to slide freely in and out of this channel without dropping out; use the same dovetail cutter to bevel off its edges. The overall length of this trammel arm is 140mm ($5\frac{1}{2}$") long, its thickness 5mm ($\frac{3}{16}$") and its width must fit the dovetailed channel – Fig. 5A.

Next, make the fence, Fig. 5A. This consists of a block 140mm × 33mm wide × 25mm thick ($5\frac{1}{2}$" × $1\frac{1}{4}$" × 1"). Drill two holes for the router's extension rods to slide through, so that the centres are the same distance apart as on the router's adjustable fence (which can be used as a template). The next step is to drill another pair of holes at right angles to the first and then chop the holes out so that you can sink a nut into each, flush with the surface; the nuts need to be fixed in with an epoxy adhesive such as 'Araldite.'

The purpose is to tighten down a pair of bolts through the holes and clamp the block at any position on the extension rods. Because the trammel arm is screwed and glued to the bottom of the block, as the latter is moved in

or out along the rods, the trammel arm goes with it. Therefore, if at the other end of the trammel arm you fix a pin (or a short length of dowel), the whole assembly will revolve around it. Any cutter inserted in the router collet will therefore describe a circle. In Fig. 7 you can see a circle 20mm ($\frac{3}{4}$") routed in this way, using a veining cutter.

There is a threaded hole on the sole-plate of the router which normally accepts the guide bush, and the slide can be bolted into this with a countersunk-head bolt. To make the assembly rigid, you can bolt a small right-angled metal strip to the other end of the slide, with another bolt screwed into the existing hole on the body of the router. One last point, the router has to be kept level while working; to achieve this, bolt a wooden strip, of the same thickness as the dovetailed slide, on the other side of the aperture in the sole-plate where a hole is provided. The circles for the inlays are made with a veining cutter to a depth of about 4mm ($\frac{3}{16}$"). If you intend to inlay the circles with a contrasting wood then this should be done next. I personally use a wood filler which is explained a little later.

We are coming to the final stages now. Continue by cutting the circular holes for the instruments – most easily done with a jigsaw. It's often necessary to rout a shallow rebate around the holes, on the rear side of the board, to accommodate the back cover plates, this can be done with the appropriate rebate cutter, with its guide pin located on the inside edge of the hole.

After thoroughly glasspapering, apply a coat of light oak stain. This kills the redness of the sapele and imparts a warm nut-brown colour. Next, brush on a coat of polyurethane matt varnish diluted 10% with white spirit; this coat is lightly papered down when dry and is followed by another (undiluted) coat and allowed to dry.

To fill the inlays I used cream-coloured wood-filler: if you are careful you can wipe away any surplus with a damp cloth – the fact that the wood has been varnished prevents the filler from entering the grain. Finally, another coat of varnish is applied and lightly papered down when dry, followed by a buffing with wax polish on a soft, lint-free cloth. The board is now finished and ready for the instruments to be affixed.

Suitable sets of instruments can be obtained from: The Art Veneer Co Ltd, Industrial Estate, Mildenhall, Suffolk IP28 7AY; or Charles Greville & Co Ltd, Willey Mill House, Alton Road, Farnham, Surrey GU10 5EL.

2. House Sign Made with a Router

Steve Watson

In this project I aim to show that a router can be a very useful tool in producing hand-made house signs with character. Wood is an ideal material as each piece has unique structure and grain markings. It is noticeable without being obtrusive and gives a warm, homely feeling.

House signs can vary according to the property and can be simply names or names decorated with leaves or acorns and the like and finished off with conventional gouges and chisels.

For the sign shown in the photograph I chose a suitable piece of oak. If possible it should be quarter-sawn for extra stability in outside conditions and at least 20 mm ($\frac{3}{4}''$) thick. Plane the top of the wood so that the router can move smoothly over the surface.

Since spacing letters is often a matter of trial and error it pays to draw the outline of the sign full size on a large sheet of paper. On a separate sheet draw out the letters in dark ink. If a letter is repeated it only needs to be drawn once. Place the letters behind the lay-out sheet and trace each one in turn after moving the letters around to find the right spacing. Letters with rounded tops such as O's, C's and S's should be slightly taller than other letters. If they are left at the same height they will look

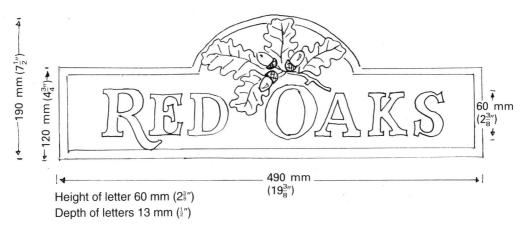

Height of letter 60 mm (2⅜″)
Depth of letters 13 mm (½″)

Fig. 1 Draw a rough outline of the design, full size, on a sheet of paper

shorter.

In choosing an appropriate lettering style do not be confined to calligraphy books. Everyday we are surrounded by the creative use of lettering on book covers, advertisements, magazines, food packaging, and so on. Look at everything and decide what you like. For 'Red Oaks' I've chosen fairly thick capital letters; the rounded corners on the serifs lend themselves well to routing.

When the name has been drawn out pin it to the wall and look at it from a distance to see if the spacing works. If you are satisfied, measure out the middle of the word and draw

a centre line. From this construct the top curve and pencil in the outline of the decoration. In this case, I did not want the acorns and oak leaves to look as though they were glued on to the sign so I made them overlap the border and hang down into the gap between the words.

Transfer the design onto the wood using carbon paper. Go over the lines with a dark, felt-tip pen then shade in with a different colour the areas to be routed so that you know exactly which side of the lines to rout. Do not cut out the outline of the sign until later as the waste wood around the outside is useful for

Fig. 2 Mark out and transfer the design to your prepared piece of wood

41

clamping the sign firmly as well as to support the base of the router.

Start by routing the smaller areas between the letters and leave the large areas until last. Take two or three shallow passes before reaching the desired depth — in this case 13 mm ($\frac{1}{2}''$). Leave plenty of space around the outside of the letters to give you room to practise the passes for the finishing cuts. Use the largest diameter router bit which will fit in the space available as it is difficult to cut straight and curved lines with small bits. When cutting the inside and outside of the 'O', for instance, I used a 15 mm ($\frac{5}{8}''$) diameter router bit.

For extra control hold the router with your hands flat on the wood and the thumb and

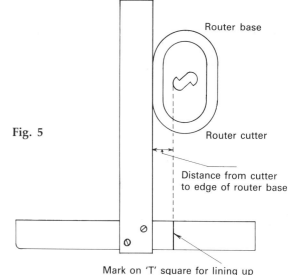

Fig. 5

Router base

Router cutter

Distance from cutter to edge of router base

Mark on 'T' square for lining up cutting line

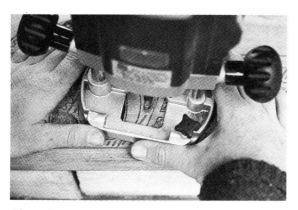

Fig. 3 Pierce the design in the waste areas to begin the cutting out

Fig. 4 Clear the waste areas around the letters

index finger of each hand around the outside of the base of the router. Remember that the wood will burn if the router speed is set too high and the rate of feed too low. Start off with a slow speed setting and gradually build it up as you get more confident.

When routing straight vertical lines use a tee-square as a guide. This can be made by screwing two straight edged pieces of plywood together to form a 90 degree angle. The head of the 'T' hooks over the edge of the sign and the tail can then be used as a guide for the router. Find the distance from the actual cutting edge of the router bit to the outside flat edge of the router base and then mark this on the head of the 'T'. The tee-square can then be clamped to the sign with the mark on the head level with the line to be routed. (As shown in the diagram Fig. 5.)

The straight horizontal lines can now be routed using the router's adjustable side guide. This is particularly useful for finishing the inside edges of the sign's raised border. It can also be used for the tops and bottoms of the letters to give them uniformity in height. However, be careful to leave the rounded letters slightly bigger than the rest.

42

Fig. 6 Continue until the main parts of the waste have been cut away

Fig. 7 Detail of Fig. 6 with the cutters used

Fig. 8 Cut out the letter centres with the small cutter, keeping the router base firmly on the board for continued support and accuracy. Leave the area below straight edged letters for finishing with the fence attachment. (See Fig. 10)

Fig. 9 Detail shows oak leaves cut out with the small cutter

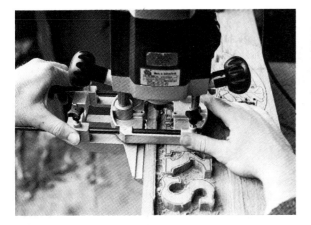

Fig. 10 Use the side fence for support when working near the edge of the board

Fig. 12 Clean up, trim and shape all the letters, leaves, etc

Rout the shape of the acorn leaves using a 4 mm ($\frac{3}{16}''$) diameter router bit with a long cutting edge. Where the leaves overlap the border rout to a depth of 4 mm ($\frac{3}{16}''$) around their edges. Now the whole of the border can be routed to this depth using the letters and the waste remaining can be attached to the outside of the sign to support the router. The leaves and the acorns can then be carved.

Texture the background with a small gouge using short scooping movements. Do not be concerned about damaging the corners of the letter as once the background is finished the edges of the letters can be bevelled using a very sharp No. 2 gouge. If the letters have been routed so that the felt-tip pen lines are still visible on their tops, the inside edges of the pen lines provide a useful guide as to how wide to make the bevels on the letters.

Finally cut out the sign and sand before either varnishing with a good quality outdoor varnish or applying numerous coats of teak oil. The screw holes can be drilled as shown, or glass plates fixed to the back of the sign.

Once the sign is fixed on the wall you can sit back and wait for it to mature and age gracefully as time passes.

Fig. 11 The panel ready for cutting to size and hand finishing with gouges

Fig. 13 A selection of house signs by Steve Watson: *Oakfield 99* has routed letters and numbers with some of the centre waste being routed out before the squirrel, leaves and acorns were hand finished. Much of the background and shaping around the number *26* and daffodil was achieved with the router. *55* has a tooled background similar to that mentioned in the project. *The Coppice* is a good example of free style lettering with acorns and leaves. *White Cottage, 867,* and *Hillcrest* show examples of colouring in the letters and numbers. *Churchill* shows a Gothic style lettering example and *Oaklands* an example of the raised lettering achieved with the use of the router as demonstrated in this project

45

3. Two-bottle Tantalus

Max Cooper

IT IS always the case that batch production takes a lot of thought and time to make the jigs necessary for doing very simple tasks; when making only a small number of an item batch production preparation is seldom worthwhile as such operations can be done quicker by hand without the aid of a jig.

This principle certainly applies when using the router for batch production work. It requires patient setting up, but once set will cut both quickly and accurately as many items as required.

I have made many tantaluses by the methods described below, and from similar jigs many things can be made by using the same techniques such as pierced book shelf ends, fretted galleries, pierced splats for chair backs.

Fixing the Router onto a Radial Arm Saw

Small radial arm saws are now widely available and found in many small workshops and, in many cases, can be adapted to take the hand router. The brackets which are available for the different models of radial arm saw usually only cater for one make of router and a feasibility study must be carried out first.

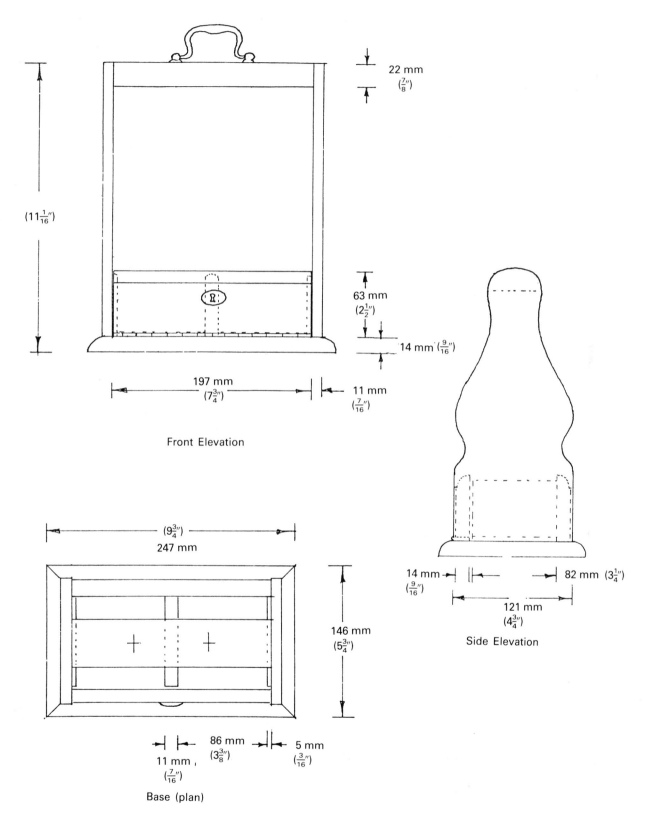

$(11\frac{1}{16}'')$

22 mm
$(\frac{7}{8}'')$

63 mm
$(2\frac{1}{2}'')$

14 mm $(\frac{9}{16}'')$

197 mm
$(7\frac{3}{4}'')$

11 mm
$(\frac{7}{16}'')$

Front Elevation

$(9\frac{3}{4}'')$
247 mm

146 mm
$(5\frac{3}{4}'')$

11 mm
$(\frac{7}{16}'')$

86 mm
$(3\frac{3}{8}'')$

5 mm
$(\frac{3}{16}'')$

Base (plan)

14 mm
$(\frac{9}{16}'')$

82 mm $(3\frac{1}{4}'')$

121 mm
$(4\frac{3}{4}'')$

Side Elevation

47

When a suitable bracket has been acquired, the saw is removed and the yoke is locked into position. The router is fixed onto the yoke and a 6mm ($\frac{1}{4}''$) straight tungsten cutter is fitted into the collet. Directly below this, into the chipboard table, is drilled a 6mm ($\frac{1}{4}''$) hole, into which a steel peg is fitted. It should protrude above the table 6mm ($\frac{1}{4}''$), this is the guide used against the template. A stop is fitted to the rise and fall on the radial arm, so that the router

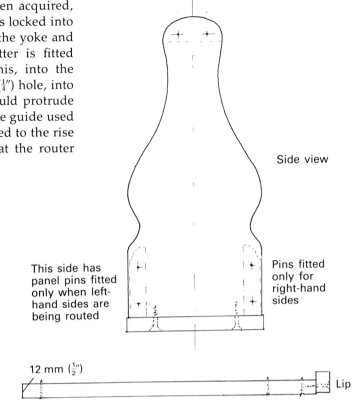

Side view

This side has panel pins fitted only when left-hand sides are being routed

Pins fitted only for right-hand sides

Fig. 1 Jig

12 mm ($\frac{1}{2}''$)

Lip

when lowered will automatically stop before the cutter hits the peg.

Make jig 1 as illustrated (Fig. 1). The shape can be re-designed to suit individual ideas. The template needs to be accurately made and the shaping finished with rasps and files. Any defect on this will be duplicated on finished pieces. Holes are drilled precisely in marked positions: two at the top and two each on either side, near the bottom. These are to take 16mm ($\frac{5}{8}''$) panel pins which go through the ply template and protrude 3mm ($\frac{1}{8}''$) on the other side. The wood to be cut out is placed against the screwed-on lip and the template fixed to it, the pins holding the work firmly for routing. When removed after routing, the side will have holes which then become centres for drilling 6mm ($\frac{1}{4}''$) dowel holes. The pair of pins on either side alternate, depending on whether it's a

right- or left-hand side, because only the back of the tantalus is fixed, the front being a hinged flap. (see diagram)

Cutting the Sides with the Router

The side blanks are roughly sawn out with a bandsaw, this reduces the amount of wood the router has to cut through and so hastens the process. The router is fixed onto jig 1, and placed face down onto the radial arm table; it is now lowered with the rise and fall handle to cut 5mm to 6mm ($\frac{3}{16}''$ to $\frac{1}{4}''$) deep; the power is switched on and the jig and blank brought up to the steel peg, with the hands guiding the work round against this peg. After one pass the router can be lowered to finish the cut. See Figs. 2 and 3.

48

Fig. 2

Fig. 3

Cutting List for each Tantalus

Item	No.	Length	Width	Thickness	Code
Base	1	247 mm $9\frac{3}{4}''$	146 mm $5\frac{3}{4}''$	14 mm $\frac{9}{16}''$	A
Sides	2	267 mm $10\frac{1}{2}''$	121 mm $4\frac{3}{4}''$	11 mm $\frac{7}{16}''$	B
Front/Back	2	197 mm $7\frac{3}{4}''$	64 mm $2\frac{1}{2}''$	14 mm $\frac{9}{16}''$	C1 and C2
Central Partition	1	82 mm $3\frac{1}{4}''$	62 mm $2\frac{7}{16}''$	11 mm $\frac{7}{16}''$	D
Top	1	197 mm $7\frac{3}{4}''$	51 mm $2''$	22 mm $\frac{7}{8}''$	E
Base Interior	2	92 mm $3\frac{5}{8}''$	87 mm $3\frac{7}{16}''$	5 mm $\frac{3}{16}''$	F
Interior of Sides	2	57 mm $2\frac{1}{4}''$	87 mm $3\frac{7}{16}''$	5 mm $\frac{3}{16}''$	G

Routing the Lock Recess and Key Hole in the Front Flap (C1)

Mark and drill a 9mm ($\frac{3}{8}''$) dia. hole at the centre top on the inside face of the front flap, 12 mm ($\frac{1}{2}''$) from the top edge and 9mm ($\frac{3}{8}''$) deep. Place this face down into the jig. Drop the jig onto the radial arm table so that the peg is in the hole; lower the router to 5mm ($\frac{3}{16}''$) below the timber surface and guide the work round the peg by hand, as shown in Figs. 4 and 5. Lower a further 3mm ($\frac{1}{8}''$) (down to prepared stop), and follow round again to finish. When this, or if applicable, the whole batch, has been completed, remove the 6mm ($\frac{1}{4}''$) router cutter and replace with a 3mm ($\frac{1}{8}''$) cutter, also replace the steel guide peg with a 3mm ($\frac{1}{8}''$) guide. (This can be drilled in a different position on the table as the yoke can be pushed back or brought forward a little.) The key hole insert can now be fitted and the key hole in the flap routed in a similar manner on the reverse side. (Figs. 6 and 7)

Figs. 4 & 5

Figs. 6 & 7

50

Moulding Base (A), Front Flap (C1) and Back (C2)

Remove the router from the radial arm saw. Fit any ovolo or ogee router cutter to suit your requirements. Fix the router beneath a router table and fence. The fence should have a plywood facing attached with a small notch cut out to allow the router cutter to fit beneath it and spin without snagging.

The parts to be moulded are the base, the front flap and the back; they are individually worked along the set fence. The direction of the feed is very important (see Fig. 8). "A" is wrong; the wood is pushed off the fence and is pulled forward out of control by the router cutter. "B" pulls work *into* the fence and relies on the work being pushed through by the operator who therefore has control.

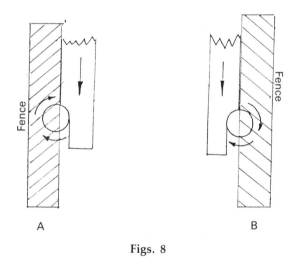

Figs. 8

Dowelling

The top rail (E) and back rail (C2) when cut to length are marked for dowelling in jigs 2a & 2b (Fig. 9). The sides having already been marked by jig 1, (E) & (C2) can now be drilled with 6mm ($\frac{1}{4}$") bit to the set depth. The top is now rounded off to come flush with the top edges of sides (B). Two holes are drilled in (E); the distance apart depends on the type of handle to be used. All parts are then sanded to satisfaction and glued together.

Base

The base, having been moulded, is now fitted into jig 3 (Fig. 10) top side down. The set panel pins in the jig mark the base for drilling screw holes. The square holes are marked round with a pencil onto the base. Impact adhesive is applied to the base within these lines and also on the base interior pieces (F), these are then placed into position when the glue has become tacky, and cramped up in the vice. A similar procedure is used on the sides and interior side pieces (G).

The marked pin holes in the base can be drilled with a 4mm ($\frac{5}{32}$") drill and countersunk on the other side. After sanding, the base can be screwed onto the completed tantalus frame, including the central partition, with 25mm (1") 6's, countersunk screws.

Complete the piece by staining, polishing and fitting all brassware. The front flap (C1), is hinged onto the tantalus with a cut-to-length piano hinge; the lock is described in the diagram. To finish, cover the base underside with felt.

JIG 1

Make from 9mm ($\frac{3}{8}$") birch plywood (multi-core). Cut to 247mm ($9\frac{3}{4}$") long and 121mm ($4\frac{3}{4}$") wide.

Draw shape onto card with centre line.
Draw and cut out shape on one half.
Use this as template to mark onto plywood with marked centre line.
Reverse card and draw round shape on the other side of centre line on the ply.
The shape is now drawn symmetrically.
Cut out and smooth edges.
Cut batten 127 × 19 × 13mm (5" × $\frac{3}{4}$" × $\frac{1}{2}$").
Screw onto the end of plywood base.
Mark lines 9mm ($\frac{3}{8}$") in from flat edges, either side of the template.
Mark centres 13mm and 44mm ($\frac{1}{2}$" and $1\frac{3}{4}$") along lines.
Mark line 248mm ($9\frac{13}{16}$") from bottom edge parallel.
Mark centres 13mm ($\frac{1}{2}$") along line, either side of centre line.
Drill holes to take 16mm ($\frac{5}{8}$") panel pins, tightly.

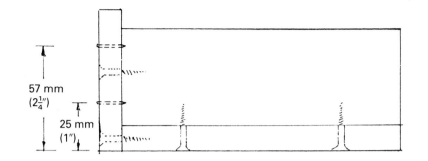

57 mm
($2\frac{1}{4}''$)

25 mm
(1")

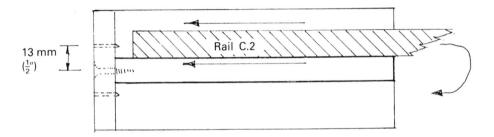

13 mm
($\frac{1}{2}''$)

Rail C.2

Fig. 9 Jig 2a

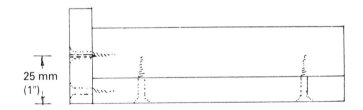

25 mm
(1")

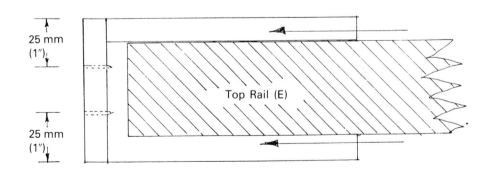

25 mm
(1")

25 mm
(1")

Top Rail (E)

Fig. 9 Jig 2b

JIG 2a (Fig. 9)

Dowelling Markers.

Make from 13mm ($\frac{1}{2}$″) plywood.

Base 152mm × 63mm (6″ × 2$\frac{1}{2}$″)
End 76mm × 63mm (3″ × 2$\frac{1}{2}$″)
Centre 152mm × 51mm (6″ × 2″)

Mark centre line down base and end.

Drill two screw holes along line.
Drill two screw holes 6mm ($\frac{1}{4}$″) from edge of end piece, and one hole along centre line.
Mark two parallel lines 13mm ($\frac{1}{2}$″) either side of centre line.
Mark off along lines 25mm and 57mm (1″ and 2$\frac{1}{4}$″), use as centres and drill to take 16mm ($\frac{5}{8}$″) panel pins.
Screw assembly together.

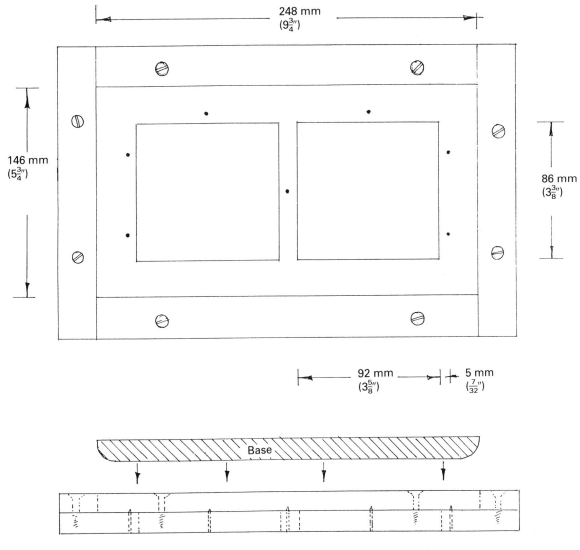

248 mm (9$\frac{3}{4}$″)

146 mm (5$\frac{3}{4}$″)

86 mm (3$\frac{3}{8}$″)

92 mm (3$\frac{5}{8}$″)   5 mm ($\frac{7}{32}$″)

Base

Fig. 10 Jig 3 For marking squares onto base and accurately marking screw holes for attaching base to frame

53

JIG 2b (Fig. 9)

Make from 13mm ($\frac{1}{2}''$) plywood.

Base 140mm × 76mm ($5\frac{1}{2}'' \times 3''$)
End 51mm × 76mm ($2'' \times 3''$)
Side 140mm × 25mm ($5\frac{1}{2}'' \times 1''$)

Drill two screw holes 6mm ($\frac{1}{4}''$) from edge of base.
Drill two screw holes 6mm ($\frac{1}{4}''$) from edge of end.
Mark line 25mm (1″) along end piece and mark two centres 25mm (1″) from either side.
Drill for 16mm ($\frac{5}{8}''$) panel pins.
Screw assembly together.

JIG 3

Cut out 9mm ($\frac{3}{8}''$) plywood, 299mm × 182mm ($11\frac{3}{4}'' \times 7\frac{3}{16}''$).

Cut wooden strips 25mm (1″) wide × 13mm ($\frac{1}{2}''$) thick and fix with screws, edges flush with plywood edge.

Cut out two rectangular holes centred with a plywood bridge of 11mm ($\frac{7}{16}''$) width dividing the two rectangles.

Drill 7 small holes 5mm ($\frac{7}{32}''$) from 3 sides of these two holes as illustrated, to take 16mm ($\frac{5}{8}''$) panel pins (tight fit is required). No panel pins are required along the front edge.

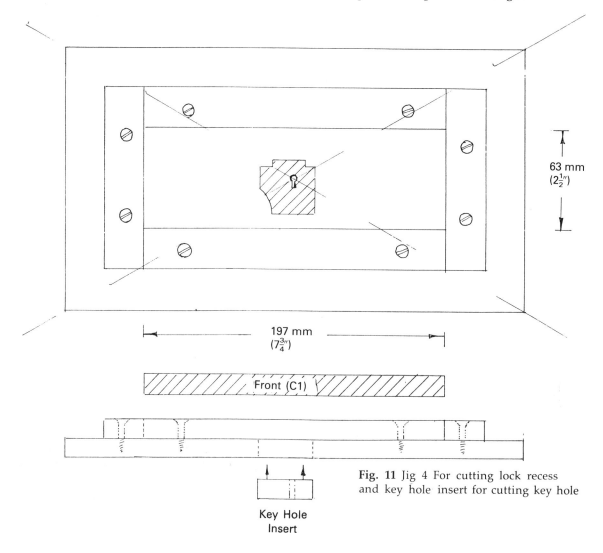

Key Hole
Insert

Fig. 11 Jig 4 For cutting lock recess and key hole insert for cutting key hole

DIAGRAM A

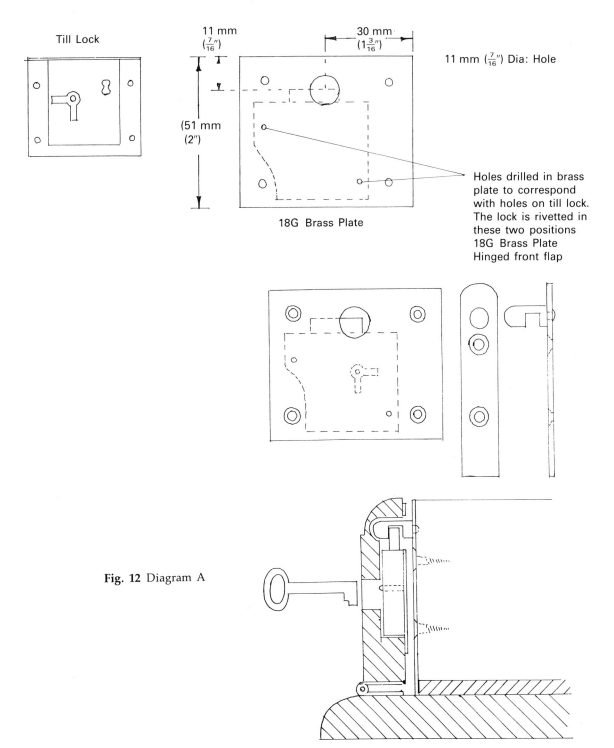

Till Lock

11 mm ($\frac{7}{16}''$)

30 mm ($1\frac{3}{16}''$)

11 mm ($\frac{7}{16}''$) Dia: Hole

(51 mm (2"))

18G Brass Plate

Holes drilled in brass
plate to correspond
with holes on till lock.
The lock is rivetted in
these two positions
18G Brass Plate
Hinged front flap

Fig. 12 Diagram A

Hinged front flap

JIG 4 (Fig. 11)

Cut 9mm ($\frac{3}{8}''$) plywood, 299mm × 165mm ($11\frac{3}{4}'' \times 6\frac{1}{2}''$).

Find centre with diagonal lines across corners.
Drill a hole the size of the lock pin.
Place lock and mark round internal casing of lock.
Cut out hole to this shape and file smooth.
Lock should now fit snugly into hole without much clearance.
Mark round inside of hole onto 9mm ($\frac{3}{8}''$) ply and cut out so that this piece fits snugly into lock recess.
Key hole is marked in correct position and is cut out of insert.

Cut 25mm (1″) wide strips.
Mark and place 25mm (1″) in from the edges of plywood and screw on.
The recess formed by the strips of wood should now hold the front flap (C1) firmly for routing.

DIAGRAM A (Fig. 12)

Purchase 38mm ($1\frac{1}{2}''$) till lock.

Brass plate and peg hook have to be made by a competent metal worker as accuracy is essential on quantity production.

Marking and drilling from two diagonal screw holes on the till lock onto the plate in correct position to the centre peg hole. Rivets are fitted through to secure the lock on the plate.

4. Sycamore Mirror Frame with Diagonal Inlay

Ramsey Pattison and Alan Smith

DESIGN inspiration for this mirror frame came from a low occasional table designed by Ramsey Pattison, which won second place in the National Student Design Awards for 1987.

The inlay design has been modified from the original, which proved very demanding in time and concentration. The table contained over 1500 pieces of inlay, complex 3-way mitred dovetails and took a year's hard work to make.

This mirror is much simpler, the frame has no joints and is cut from a single piece of medium density fibreboard. The router was used to cut out the frame perimeter, trim the waste from the centre, and rebate the back for the glass.

The inlay grooves are cut using a pair of plywood jigs, also made using the router. The inlay is black stringing made from dyed sycamore. The appearance of the inlay can be improved by bleaching it to soften the harshness of the black by soaking in a solution of household bleach and water.

List of Materials

MDF 1 piece 15 × 500 × 750mm ($\frac{5}{8}$ × 20 × 30″) to be cut to finished size 445 × 668mm (17$\frac{1}{2}$ × 26$\frac{5}{16}$″) exactly.
Sycamore veneer 1.3 sq m (13 sq ft.)
Black stringing 3mm ($\frac{1}{8}$″) square × 9 m (30 ft)

Tools and Equipment

Router
1.5mm (1/16″) and 6mm (1/4″) cutters
1.5mm (1/16″) 6mm (1/4″) and 19mm (3/4″) chisels
Mitre square, small toolmaker's square and try square
Straight edge and steel rule
Marking knife and marking gauge
Jack plane and bullnose plane
Left-hand and right-hand mitre jig
Stringing line trimming jig, cramps, scraper.

Making the Frame

A piece of MDF larger than the finished size is used so as to ensure accurate cutting to size and squaring up.

The best side of the MDF is face marked and two edges are planed straight and square. The other two edges of the frame are now marked out and the excess cut off with the router using a long 6mm (1/4″) diameter straight cutter. As always with man-made boards, a TCT cutter is recommended.

During this part of the operation the router is guided by a straight batten, clamped to the surface of the MDF. Remember to make the MDF overhang the bench, so that the router cutter can pierce it without damage.

A sharp cutter will produce a clean square edge; any stray whiskers can be removed with fine abrasive paper.

Cutting out the Middle

The finished frame width is 50mm (2″) with the veneer applied, so it must be cut less the thickness of the two pieces of veneer. The

Fig. 1 Cutting out the middle

router fence is set to give this width, and then each side of the frame is cut out in turn. Once again it is important to allow the MDF to overhang the bench, as the cutter will pass right through the board. Figure 1 shows the board receiving additional support from the bench vice as it is cut while the frame and unwanted centre panel are secured with cramps.

All the inside corners of the frame will be rounded as they come from the router cutter, they are then pared square using a chisel and guide block clamped to the surface of the MDF.

Veneering

All surfaces of the frame are veneered. The first stage is to cut oversize pieces of sycamore, sixteen in all. One end of each of the wide strips for the front and back of the frame is mitred at 45 degrees exactly, this will save time and trouble when applying the veneer.

The veneer is applied with PVA glue. On a small surface like this the veneer can be pressed down cold, using clamps and scrap wood battens to hold it flat until the glue sets. A couple of blocks cut in the shape of right angle triangles measuring 65mm ($2\frac{1}{2}''$) on the two short sides will also be useful.

Veneer for the inner edges is cut to length using the engineer's square. Trim off a sliver at a time, using the square as a guide until the length is perfect when smoothed down by hand.

When applying the veneer an exact sequence has to be followed. The inner and outer edges are done before the front and back, the short edges being done before the long ones – it looks nicer that way.   Apply veneer to one edge at a time as the frame has to be laid flat on the bench to allow surplus veneer to be trimmed off. Use a sharp and finely set jack plane for this, proceeding with caution to avoid tearing up the delicate veneer edges.

After the inner and outer edges are done, the front and back can be veneered. Before laying these use a fine hard pencil to mark in the exact position of the corner mitres.

Lay one strip at a time, coating the MDF with glue to just beyond the mitre line. Position one end of the veneer so that the pre-cut mitre is exactly on the pencil line and then smooth the whole length down. Use one of the triangular pads to press the veneer down against the mitre line. This enables any "creep" of the veneer to be seen when pressure is applied. The rest of the strip is clamped down using a rectangular strip of scrap timber.

When each strip of face veneer has set, the overhanging waste is trimmed away using the jack plane for the outer edges and the bullnose plane inside the frame. The last stage for each of the first three strips is to pare away the square end with a sharp knife and steel rule, until it exactly lines up with the pencilled mitre lines on the frame corners.

The last strip of veneer is cut to exact size before laying. It is then pressed into place using a triangular block at each end and a length of scrap between them. Any errors in the fit of the last strip must be corrected

immediately, for they will be glaringly obvious when the glue has set.

Cutting the Rebate

The size of the rebate required will vary slightly with the thickness and size of glass required. The mirror used for this project was backed with a special plastic film giving additional support. Ordinary mirror glass may require the

Fig. 2a–b Cutting the rebate

protection of a 4mm ($\frac{3}{16}$") plywood back fitted into a second, slightly larger and shallower rebate. This is made in two stages, each one identical to the single rebate described here.

Cutting the rebate is illustrated in Figure 2. The limits of the rebate are marked in with a cutting gauge; the router fence and cutter depth are then set to suit this.

When routing out the inner edge the plunge action of the router should be used continuously to "nibble" the veneer away otherwise it may be torn off. Away from the edges the router can be used in a smooth continuous motion. Once again the corners must be squared up by hand.

Cutting the Inlay Grooves

Begin by marking out the inlay grooves as shown in the diagram. The bridging line at each end of the closed space between adjacent lines is scored by pressing a chisel into it. Guide the chisel by clamping a straight edge along each face of the frame in turn.

Figure 3 shows the left-hand inlay groove routing jig. It is made from 9mm ($\frac{3}{8}$") plywood and is 400 mm (16") long and 150mm (6") wide. In use it is clamped to a straight length of wood, which in turn is clamped to the underside of the frame. Another jig is made in an exact mirror image of this for cutting right-hand mitres.

When the jigs are in use the side of the frame being worked on must overhang the edge of the bench, allowing the jig-guide batten clamps to be fastened beneath it.

Before cutting each groove, the end nearest the inside edge of the frame must be cut by plunging in the router. This will help to prevent breaking out. The cutter is raised after plunging and the machine slid forward over to the outer edge of the frame. Now the cutter is lowered and the router pushed back, cutting the groove towards the inner edge of the frame.

The width of the stringing lines can vary, so when the routing is begun make two passes with a 1.5mm ($\frac{1}{16}$") router cutter so that the groove ends up approximately 2.2m ($\frac{3}{32}$") wide. As cutting proceeds the jig will start to lift up

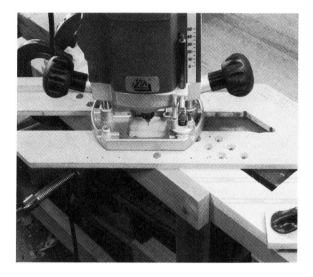

Fig. 3a–b Cutting the inlay grooves

on the whiskers that form along the edges of the grooves. These must be removed frequently by slicing off with a chisel pressed flat against the frame surface.

Cutting the Inlay Strips

The ends of the short inlay strips which fill the space between the pairs of grooves must be angled at 45 degrees before they are fitted. A look at the finished mirror (page 57) shows that there are 26 left-hand and 26 right-hand mitres.

60

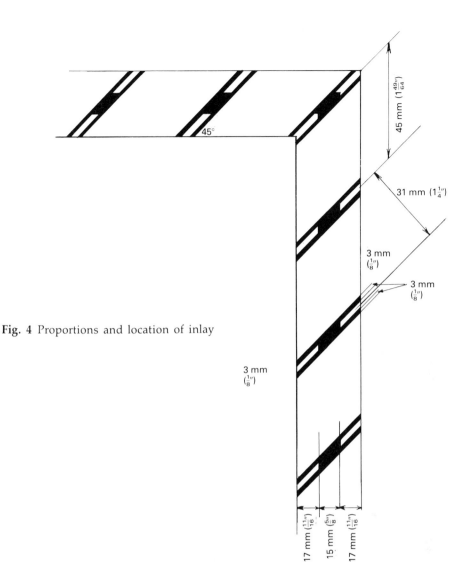

45 mm ($1\frac{49}{64}''$)

31 mm ($1\frac{1}{4}''$)

3 mm ($\frac{1}{8}''$)

3 mm ($\frac{1}{8}''$)

45°

3 mm ($\frac{1}{8}''$)

17 mm ($\frac{11}{16}''$)   15 mm ($\frac{5}{8}''$)   17 mm ($\frac{11}{16}''$)

Fig. 4 Proportions and location of inlay

The jig used to cut the mitres on the short strips is made from a thin board of hardwood with two grooves routed across it. The grooves start from the same edge, and one goes at 45 degrees to the left, and one at 45 degrees to the right. Make them around 75mm (3″) apart at their closest point and the same width and depth as the stringing.

Fix a board of 19mm ($\frac{3}{4}''$) softwood beneath the hardwood board, the same length but 25mm (1″) wider. This extra width overhangs on the side where the grooves converge. Build up the surface of the softwood enough for it to support evenly a piece of stringing placed in one of the grooves. Finally, glue another strip of hardwood

to the upper board so that it can be used as a guide fence when chopping the mitres on the stringing.

To make the angled stringing insert a piece into one of the grooves until the required length has been achieved. Steady the string with one finger and cut the surplus wood away with a 9mm ($\frac{3}{8}''$) chisel held upright against the guide fence.

Fitting the Inlay

Each piece of inlay is fitted individually. Start by gluing in one of the long strips in each pair of grooves, then fit the short strip in the centre,

61

and finally glue in the last side of the pair. Do this pair-by-pair, working steadily around the frame.

If the grooves seem tight they may be pared very carefully with a marking knife. The strips must fit in place snugly. The short inlays will need marking for length individually and one end re-mitred with a chisel. The stringing is held in by a tiny smear of glue along each groove and, if necessary, the short inlay is pushed up tight against the long strips with tiny wedges until the glue that holds it in place has set. Often the short inlay will need to be reduced in width slightly so that the final long inlay strip in each pair slides neatly into place.

Finish the inlaying by trimming off the overhanging ends of the long strips. A convenient way to do this is to clamp a length of softwood to the face of the mirror, overhanging one edge. This can be used as a backing board while the projecting stringing is cut off with a sharp chisel.

Cleaning up

A light scraping should be all that is required; sanding must be done very carefully, for unless the inlay has been bleached, the black-dyed wood dust will mark the pale sycamore groundwork. Finish by fixing the back with small screws.

5. Eighteenth-century Welsh Dresser in Oak

Harold Babb

THIS particular piece was chosen not so much for the amount of work that it offers for the router, but the challenge to do something different with this very versatile machine.

The maximum overall sizes of this dresser are 2.134m high × 1.626m wide × 0.457m deep (7'0" × 5'4" × 1'6"). The lower section has three turned legs at the front, two square legs at the back and three large drawers at the top, with three small spice drawers below. The upper part has three shelves with plate grooves and a top.

The mouldings and housings for shelves are the usual straightforward router work as are the rebates in the back of the upper section to receive back boards. These are rebated on alternate edges to form half lap joints.

The interesting part begins with the two arches and gets even better when forming sinkings for the cocked beads where great care is needed to avoid overruns at intersections. However, more of this later.

Construction Notes for the Upper Part

The sides are tenoned into the shoes and these in turn are dowelled to the top of the base unit.

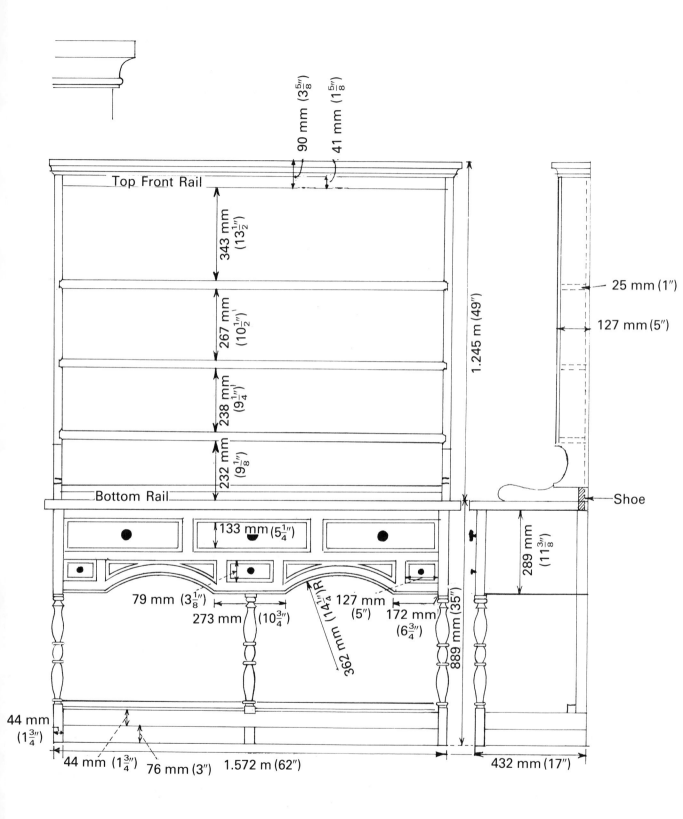

90 mm ($3\frac{5}{8}$")
41 mm ($1\frac{5}{8}$")

Top Front Rail

343 mm ($13\frac{1}{2}$")

267 mm ($10\frac{1}{2}$")

238 mm ($9\frac{1}{4}$")

232 mm ($9\frac{1}{8}$")

Bottom Rail

133 mm ($5\frac{1}{4}$")

79 mm ($3\frac{1}{8}$")
273 mm ($10\frac{3}{4}$")
362 mm ($14\frac{1}{4}$")R
127 mm (5")
172 mm ($6\frac{3}{4}$")

1.245 m (49")

25 mm (1")
127 mm (5")

Shoe

289 mm ($11\frac{3}{8}$")

889 mm (35")

44 mm ($1\frac{3}{4}$")
44 mm ($1\frac{3}{4}$")
76 mm (3")
1.572 m (62")
432 mm (17")

Welsh Dresser

Side members
rebated
for back boards

Back boards half lapped together glued and pinned to bottom rail

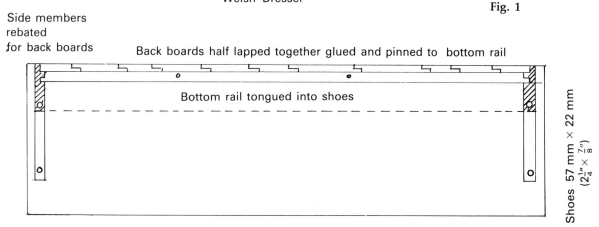

Bottom rail tongued into shoes

Shoes 57 mm × 22 mm ($2\frac{1}{4}'' \times \frac{7}{8}''$)

The sides and shoes are of 22mm ($\frac{7}{8}''$) material as are the shelves. The back is of 6mm ($\frac{1}{4}''$) random width boards – a very good opportunity to use up some of your offcuts. On the front edges of the shelves and sides, small round-edged cover fillets are applied so that the shelf housings are able to go right across the side members or rout out stopped housings if preferred. The front top rail is half lapped over the sides and top, standing forward to match up with cover fillets on the sides and shelves. Cover fillets are 25 × 5mm ($1'' \times \frac{3}{16}''$) rounded on both sides and mitred at joints. The bottom rail is set in flush with a rebate, and the back

boards run right down over it, with two dowels equally spaced to prevent the back moving outwards.

The Base Unit

The base unit has three turned legs at the front with the straight stretcher tenoned into outer legs and half lapped into centre leg. The centre leg stops below the small drawer and is tenoned into the shaped rail. The back stretcher is glued and screwed to the rear legs on top of the side rails.

Front

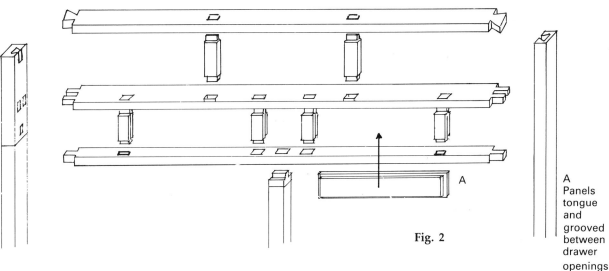

A

A
Panels
tongue
and
grooved
between
drawer
openings

Fig. 2

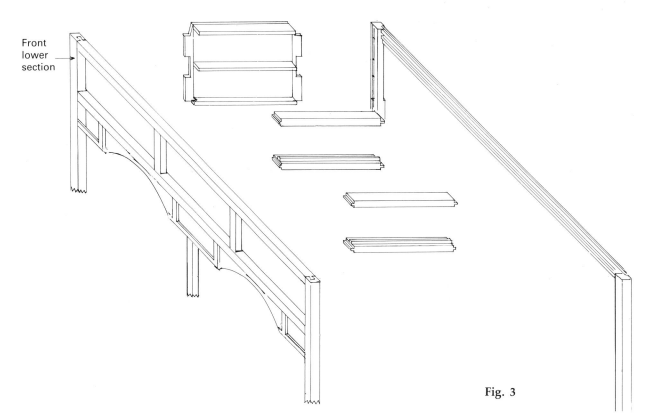

Front
lower
section →

Fig. 3

The front is made up of a bottom rail 25 × 25mm (1″ × 1″), middle rail 25 × 44mm (1″ × 1¾″), four muntins 25 × 25mm (1″ × 1″) with two panels 25mm (1″) thick, tongued and grooved in between drawer openings, cutting the shoulders on the face side 3mm (⅛″) short for cocked beads. (Figs. 2 and 3) The bottom rail has single

tenons into the end legs; the middle rail is laid flat with double tenons jointed into legs. The top rail, again, is laid flat and dovetailed into tops of legs with two 51mm (2″) muntins between the drawers. Drawer runners are slotted into the back of the bottom and middle rails. Prepare and make up the lower section

Fig. 4 Second cut of arc in progress to form rebate for cocked bead

Fig. 5 Groove for cocked bead

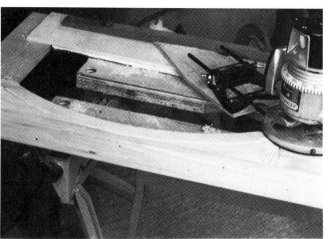

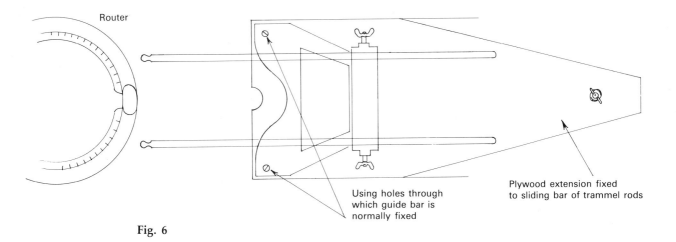

Router

Using holes through
which guide bar is
normally fixed

Plywood extension fixed
to sliding bar of trammel rods

Fig. 6

and clean off; you are now ready to form the arches and sinkings for cocked beads.

The method I have found to give the best results for this work is to fix a rigid framework to the back of the middle rail with spacing pieces behind the bottom rail and crosspiece to allow an arc of 361mm (14$\frac{1}{4}$″) radius to be struck through the points indicated on the front elevation. This is readily obtained by taking the central points between the lower drawers and squaring them down over the crosspiece

Fig. 7 Groove for straight bead

on the jig. Then mark the measurements given on the drawing to determine where the arc strikes out at the bottom of the rail. It is then a matter of measuring from these points to the centre line to obtain the radius point. (Figs. 4, 5, & 7).

You will probably find, as I did, that the trammel rods on your router are not long enough, but I found that a piece of 6mm ($\frac{1}{4}$″) ply attached to the crosspiece on the rods in place of the fence, with a small bolt and nut through the ply and crosspiece on the jig, proved very satisfactory. (Fig. 6). The dimension given for the radius is to the bottom edge of the rail and includes the cocked bead, so that it is easier to increase the setting by the thickness of the cocked bead, 3mm ($\frac{1}{8}$″), using a 13mm ($\frac{1}{2}$″) straight router bit set to cut 10mm ($\frac{3}{8}$″) deep; cut both arcs, then reset to cut through the full thickness at 3mm ($\frac{1}{8}$″) less radius, this will provide the recess for the cocked bead.

To obtain the setting for the second arc, put in a 3mm ($\frac{1}{8}$″) straight cutter and place the router back on the jig, then reset the trammel so that outer edge of the cutter reaches the lower edge of the middle rail. It is important that this rail is not cut into, otherwise the straight section that intersects will be out of line with the beads on the top edges of the drawers.

Having completed the arcs, reassemble the router and work over from the top edge of the centre rail to form a groove for the straight

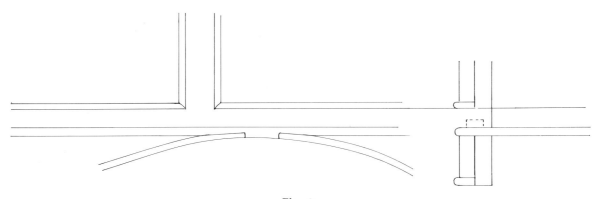

Fig. 8

section by placing the tool on the work with the bit in the top of arc, and set the fence up to the rail. Take great care not to overrun when running into the end grooves.

Choose a contrasting wood for the cocked beads and drawer knobs to make the most of the design. When fitting the beads to the insets, fit the straight ones at the top first, then, to make the joints at intersections with radiused pieces, it will be necessary to form a splice to allow rounded edges to follow through on the under edge as shown in Fig. 8.

Complete the upper portion of the front frame and prepare the legs, keeping the turning fairly simple and in keeping with the rest of the dresser. Form mortises for front and side members and finish assembling the front. Prepare side rails and plain legs for the back, using double haunched tenons on wide top rails.

It was normal practice to use a skeleton frame at the back to support runners and guides for drawers, but it is much easier to use a solid timber back (although rather extravagant), or a

Back

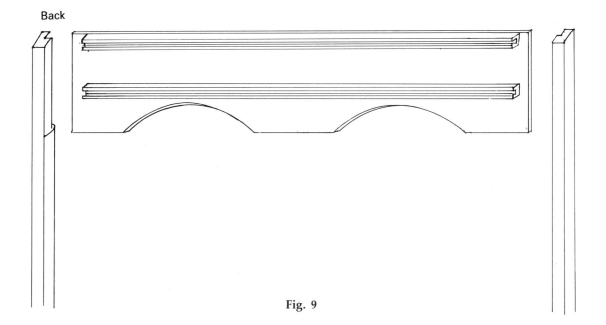

Fig. 9

68

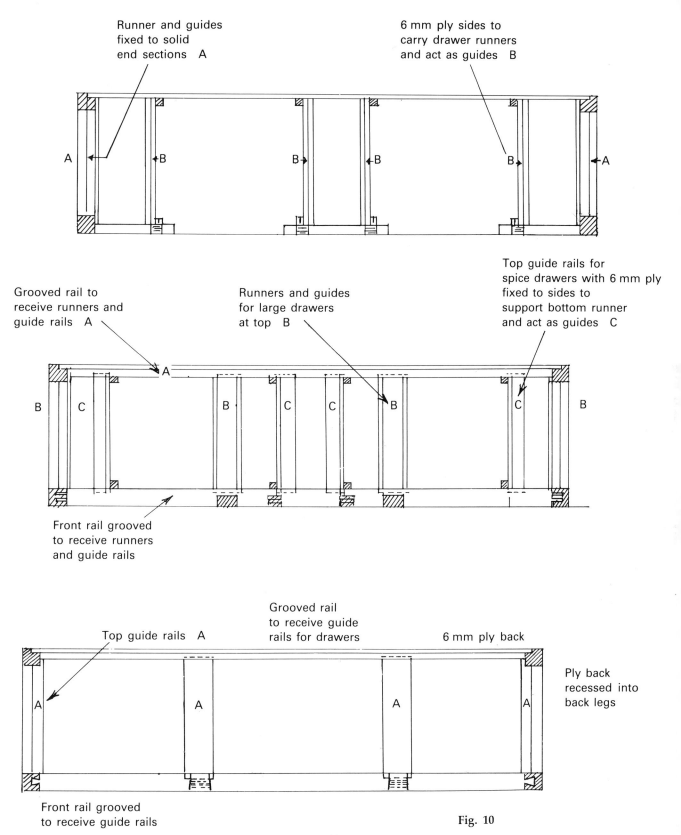

Runner and guides fixed to solid end sections A

6 mm ply sides to carry drawer runners and act as guides B

A ← →B B→ ←B B→ ←A

Grooved rail to receive runners and guide rails A

Runners and guides for large drawers at top B

Top guide rails for spice drawers with 6 mm ply fixed to sides to support bottom runner and act as guides C

B C B C C B C B

Front rail grooved to receive runners and guide rails

Top guide rails A

Grooved rail to receive guide rails for drawers

6 mm ply back

Ply back recessed into back legs

A A A A

Front rail grooved to receive guide rails

Fig. 10

69

Dovetailing
with router
using jig

Cocked
bead

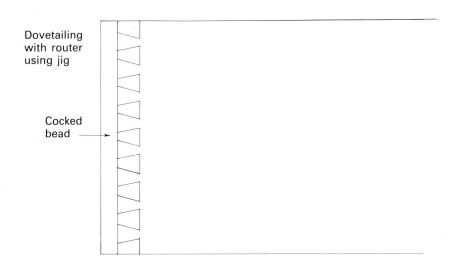

Fig. 11

Section
through
drawer

Cocked
beads
glued into
rebates in
edges of
drawers
standing
proud of
front

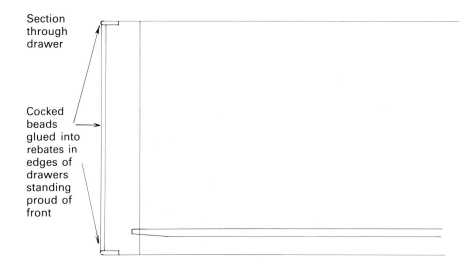

Fig. 12

6mm ($\frac{1}{4}''$) plywood back, cut to match the shape of the front (Fig. 9). If you decide on the plywood, it will need to be recessed into the back legs before assembly. Two 25 × 19mm (1″ × $\frac{3}{4}''$) rails are prepared with a groove in one side to receive runners and guides and are glued and pinned to the ply back, corresponding to the positions of the middle and top rails of the front frame. Rails can also be fixed between to carry the framework for the spice drawers below. (Fig. 10)

Having completed the carcase of the base, fit drawer fronts and construct drawers using stopped dovetails on fronts with through dovetails for backs. These can be made with a router dovetail attachment if you have one (Fig. 11). Keep the backs above drawer bottoms to allow stops to be fixed on rails of front frame. Make sure that the depth of the drawers from front to back is less than depth of the carcase to prevent damage to the back. When all drawers are fitted to slide in and out easily, set up the router to rebate the edges of drawers on all sides to receive cocked beads. These should stand slightly above the edges and taper down level on the inner edge, so that when the drawer is closed, the opening is completely filled. (Fig. 12)

Turn the drawer knobs with their own dowel so that no fixing shows: three 51mm (2″) diameter ones for large drawers and three 30mm (1$\frac{1}{4}''$) diameter ones for spice drawers, keeping the profiles fairly flat. (Fig. 13)

The last structural job is to prepare and fix the top which is 1626 × 457 × 22mm thick (5′4″ × 1′6″ × $\frac{7}{8}''$); this is screwed down through the bottoms of the dowel holes that also receive dowels in the shoes of the upper section. Take care not to drill dowel holes too deep, 13mm ($\frac{1}{2}''$) is sufficient.

Drill screw holes through top front rail in the centre of each drawer opening and screw up through the rail into the underside of the top. This way no fixing shows.

Ideally, the finish should be stain and wax polish. Alternatively you may like to try using one coat of medium oak stain then one coat of gloss polyurethane, followed by one coat of semi-gloss polyurethane. The latter method answers quite well when time is limited, although I prefer the wax finish as it does justice to the oak in bringing out its true beauty.

Note All sizes given are finished sizes.

Fig. 13 Front of large drawer and side of spice drawer

Some alternative suggestions for the display of your indoor plants using the router

(*Sketch by courtesy of Ian Norbury*)

6. Plant Stand

Fraser Budd

THIS project is a solution to a design brief describing the need to display indoor plants in an attractive and unusual way. It may stand on the floor or on a table top. In addition to the example shown, a fourth arm may be added to complete the two-way symmetry of design, more suitable when displayed away from the wall.

When selecting a suitable timber, choose a hardwood which works and finishes well and cleanly.

The joints employed have been selected for a variety of reasons, an important one being to make the final assembly and gluing operation

as simple as possible without the need for cramps.

To begin the project one should first produce the turned components i.e. the ball and three cylindrical barrels. Turn the ball first. Two spigots need to be formed to project from the centres on either side. These are the plugs onto which the barrels fit and must correspond exactly to the size of boring cutter available, recommended size 19 mm ($\frac{3}{4}$"). The third spigot is produced by boring into the ball and inserting a separately turned plug pre-cut to length. If this plug is not glued in immediately the ball may be given its final clean up on the

73

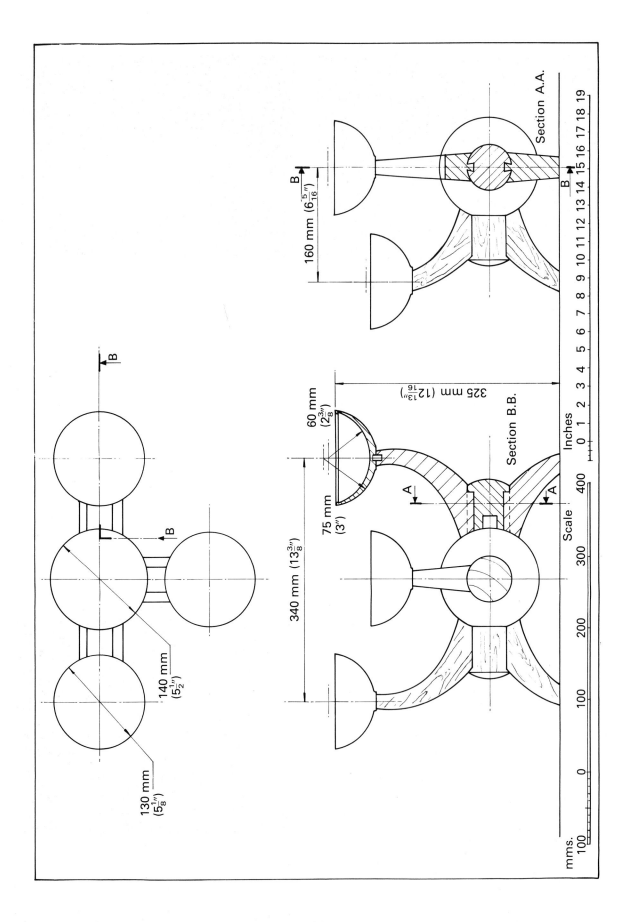

140 mm
$(5\frac{1}{2}")$

130 mm
$(5\frac{1}{8}")$

B

160 mm $(6\frac{5}{16}")$

Section A.A.

Inches

0 1 2 3 4 5 6 7 8 9 10 11 12 13 14 15 16 17 18 19

60 mm
$(2\frac{3}{8}")$

75 mm
(3")

340 mm $(13\frac{3}{8}")$

325 mm $(12\frac{13}{16}")$

Section B.B.

Scale

A

0   100   200   300   400

mms.
100

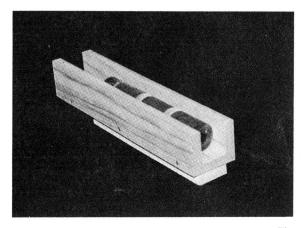

Fig. 1a–b

lathe prior to assembly.

The barrels should be turned as one piece allowing at least 20–25mm ($\frac{3}{4}$"–1") between each. (These spaces are important during the routing procedure.) Carefully check the diameter with callipers; even small dimensional differences will create problems later when it is intended that the router will need readjusting as few times as possible; each of the arms will fit any of the six housings.

The lengths must be accurately marked and the curve of the ends roughly shaped. Cut away the waste between the barrels making sure the final diameter is less than that of the ball spigots. In order that the circumference of the barrels can meet the surface of the ball the joining ends must be undercut to accommodate the curve of the ball.

Before one can commence routing, a simple jig needs to be produced. (See Fig. 1.) It is important that the cylinder fits tight into the box and the top two edges need to be parallel and level. (If you have a thicknesser the jig may be passed through this to achieve the result.) The sides should allow the router base to just clear the cylinder. When in use the router fence must be clear of the bench top with the jig tightly clamped in the vice, this is important if the cylinder is to be held in place against the considerable pull to one side exerted by the router cutter. Slipping will result in a crooked cut. To assist setting up in the vice it is helpful to attach a thicknessing block to the underside of the jig.

Before routing the dovetail housings, the tool must be set to cut a slot 12mm ($\frac{1}{2}$") deep, into the cylinder. The recommended cutter for this is the Trend 31/3 Dovetail cutter. A single cut with this size tool will result in a rather narrow slot; to remedy this, mark a line with a marking gauge 6mm ($\frac{1}{4}$") on either side of a centre line along the barrel. (See Fig. 2.)

Finally, mark a clear line to indicate the end of the slot. When using the dovetail cutter one has no alternative but to cut directly to the finished depth. However, if the reader is unhappy about so heavy a cut then the slot may be pre-routed using a smaller straight cutter.

To achieve the desired 12mm ($\frac{1}{2}$") wide slot two cuts need to be made; the first should be

Fig. 2

Fig. 3

to the line nearest the fence, this will prevent the cutter pulling away from you.

Before switching on, check the following:

1. The cutter lateral setting.
2. Depth setting.
3. That the fence locking screws are tight.
4. The stop line.
5. That the vice is tight.

Now, produce the first cut (See Figs. 3 & 4). This can be done using the spaces between the

Fig. 4

barrels to place the cutter prior to each cut. Set the cutter to the remaining line and repeat. The cylinder can now be released and twisted round ready to cut the remaining slots exactly opposite the first. When finished, the ends of the slots can be squared-up with a chisel.

Saw the barrels apart and trim off the stumps of waste wood. Using an engineer's centre-square, accurately mark the centres for boring the holes which join the barrels to the ball. To bore the holes mount the cutter (preferably a Forstener bit) in the pillar drill and set up the barrels as shown in Fig. 5 using the jig box as a clamp. (Note the use of the try square.)

Fig. 5

To make the six curved arms only one template is needed as they are all the same shape, being cut off to different lengths. On material 35mm (1⅜″) thick mark the six outlines and bandsaw or hand cut them, taking care to saw just to the waste side of the line. To leave irregular or unnecessary amounts of waste will not be helpful to the following process.

Using spokeshaves complete the shaping and finishing of one arm only and check that its curves are smooth and regular; the flat face can be planed flat and square. This arm is the master from which we can quickly produce the remaining five arms to a standard requiring only light glass-papering.

Using double-sided tape firmly fix the master to the next arm to be shaped. Set up the router with a 12mm (½″) straight cutter inverted below a routing table. A simple profiling arm can be made to fit over the tool. (See Figs. 6 & 7.) It should have a smoothly rounded end against which the master will travel. (Some router manufacturers supply a profiling arm as an accessory, however, the method used here is more adaptable and much less prone to vibration if heavy cuts are required.) The radiused end is set directly in line with the cutting edge and is positioned to touch the master, (Fig. 6). With a depth of cut of about 10mm ($\frac{3}{8}$″) it should be simple to copy the master. This can be repeated to each arm in turn. The master is no longer required as a template. The profiling arm should now be moved down to the position shown in Fig. 7, contacting only with the routed area, enabling the cutter to remove the waste below it in one or two cuts. (Care must be taken to feed in the right direction, i.e. *against* the direction of the cutter: it is extremely dangerous to get this wrong.)

All that remains is to complete the dovetail. Mark the middle of the arm and, holding the

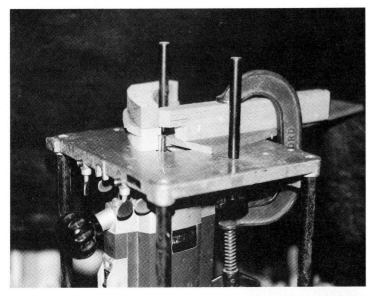

Fig. 6

Fig. 7

Fig. 8

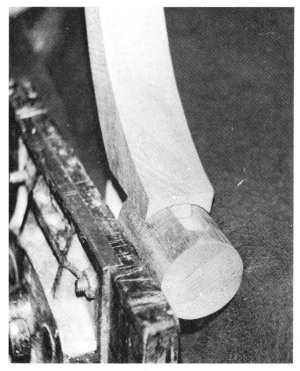

Fig. 9

barrel in place over it, scribe into the joint and around the shoulders. (See Fig. 8.) The circular saw can be set to cut along the lines to form the pins, take care the kerf does not go beyond the shoulder line. Much of the waste can be removed with the router cutting into the saw kerf and trimming to the shoulder line, for this operation use the router under its table with a fence.

The final fitting must be done using a paring gouge with a curve as near to that of the barrel as possible. With careful paring and testing, a perfect fit will be achieved. The arm will not slide in over the dovetail stop until the back end of the pin has been cut away and shaped to the curve of the barrel. (See Figs. 9 & 10.)

The final stage to complete the structure ready for cleaning and assembly is to finish the still-rough ends of the barrels. The blank end needs to go back on the lathe. To hold these, a simple face-plate clamp can be made as illustrated in Fig. 11. The split in the clamp must be made along the grain, and the hole to retain the barrel, bored out while on the lathe.

This device will hold the barrel firmly whilst the end is shaped to a smooth, shallow dome.

Fit the arms and barrels together and locate the latter onto the spigots. To achieve a perfect joint between the arm and the ball, scribe lines onto the arm keeping parallel to the curve of the ball. Carefully pare back to the lines,

Fig. 10

undercutting to accommodate the curve of the ball.

The three small bowls should be turned as thinly as possible and located onto the arms using dowels.

Clean up all the parts and carefully glue and assemble. Check the alignment of the arms and leave to harden; cramps should not be necessary. If any joints are found to be loose the application of cramps will be very awkward.

A water resistant finish should be applied. Rubbing in several coats of petroleum jelly will bring out the character of the wood and repel any water which may be spilled. The bowls need a waterproof lining, this may be achieved using paint or varnish or, best of all, if the reader has access to a vacuum forming machine, plastic liners can be moulded to exactly fit and may be held in by contact adhesive.

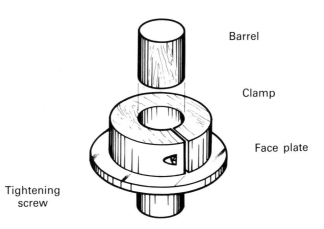

Fig. 11 A simple base plate clamp to finish the barrel ends

7. Canterbury

Mehmet Djemal

CANTERBURYS first appeared around the early 1800's and it was suggested by Sheraton that the name came from the Archbishop of Canterbury who ordered the first one. They were ideally designed to carry the large music sheets and portfolios of the day and as such were very much part of the music- or sitting-room furniture. It was usual to have a drawer under the music sheet rack; the canterbury was made with small casters so that it could be moved easily between instruments, players or rooms. In Victorian times the designs became very ornate, the canterburys were much heavier and their popularity later declined.

By far the most pleasing design was that made in the Georgian period from which this design has been adapted. Today, canterburys serve excellently as newspaper and magazine racks. When made from a good hardwood, such as mahogany, their delicate lines would enhance any home.

This canterbury has been designed to be made almost entirely with the router and router table; this cuts down the degree of difficulty and labour to a minimum.

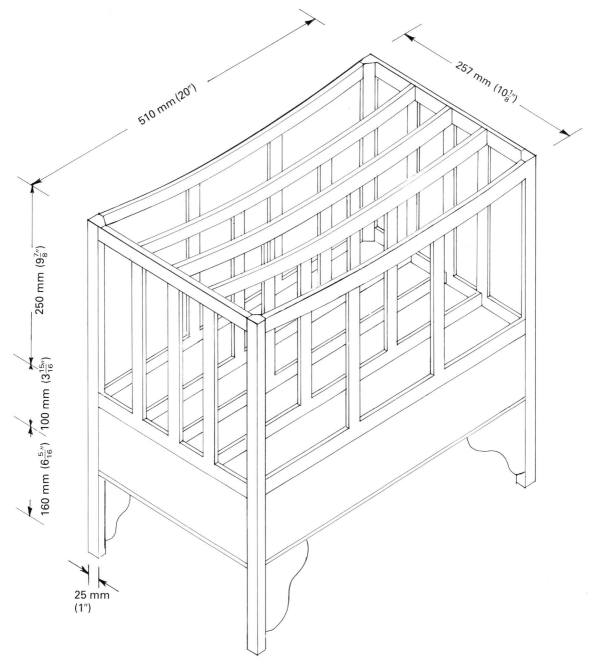

510 mm (20")

257 mm ($10\frac{1}{8}$")

250 mm ($9\frac{7}{8}$")

100 mm ($3\frac{15}{16}$")

160 mm ($6\frac{5}{16}$")

25 mm
(1")

Construction of the Top Frame

Mortise and tenon joints are used to construct the frame which forms the top part of the canterbury. Mortises are cut with the router by holding the workpiece clamped in a bench vice with the surface parallel to the bench top. A slot is cut 6mm ($\frac{1}{4}$") at a time until the required depth is achieved.

Tenons are cut with the router inverted and mounted underneath the router table. The cutter used for this operation has a bottom cut, and is set to protrude vertically to the thickness of the tenon. The mitre fence, with the rail held firmly against it, is moved forward so that the rail end is trimmed by the cutter on all four sides of the rail until the tenon is formed. Once

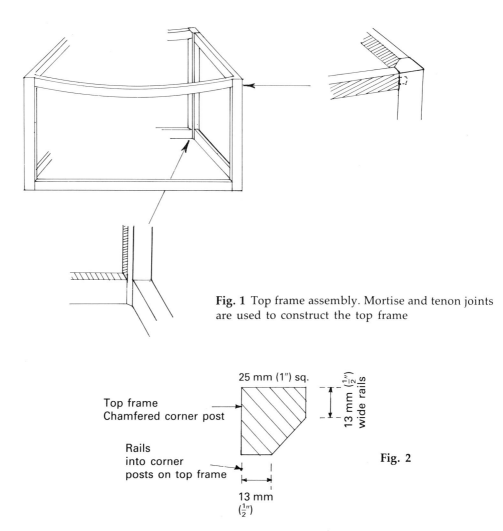

Fig. 1 Top frame assembly. Mortise and tenon joints are used to construct the top frame

Top frame
Chamfered corner post →

Rails
into corner
posts on top frame →

25 mm (1″) sq.

13 mm ($\frac{1}{2}$″) wide rails

13 mm ($\frac{1}{2}$″)

Fig. 2

the outside frame has been constructed, three vertical division frames are made by the same method and fitted inside the box construction. They can be glued into position as both side and end members are face grain.

Four slats form the floor in between the vertical divisions. They are joined in on all four sides by means of loose tongue and grooves cut by the groover, as used for the carcase sides. The completed frame is later screwed to the carcase from inside the top of the carcase.

Carcase Construction

The carcase sides and back are loose tongue and groove jointed onto the corner posts. This

is achieved by fitting a grooving cutter to a router which is inverted and fitted underneath the router table.

The carcase front rails are gauged to the thickness of the dovetail required, then marked on the corner posts and lap dovetailed as shown in the drawing. Four drawer runners are fitted and secured with two screws on each. Joining the back of the runners to the back of the carcase with simple mortise and tenon joints makes the carcase much more rigid.

Drawer Construction

Using a dovetail jig, the drawer front is clamped horizontally and the drawer side vertically onto

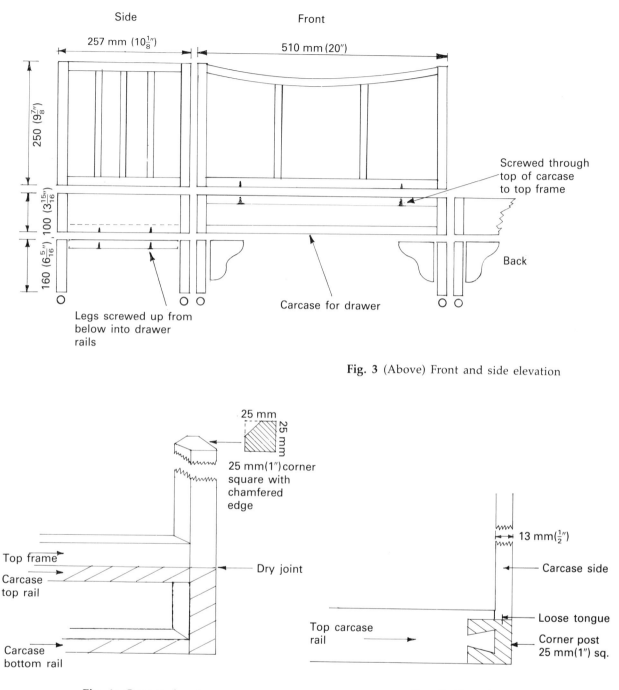

Side   Front

257 mm (10⅛″)

510 mm (20″)

250 (9⅞″)

100 (3 15/16″)

160 (6 5/16″)

Screwed through top of carcase to top frame

Back

Legs screwed up from below into drawer rails

Carcase for drawer

Fig. 3 (Above) Front and side elevation

25 mm

25 mm

25 mm (1″) corner square with chamfered edge

Top frame

Carcase top rail

Dry joint

Carcase bottom rail

Fig. 4a Carcase drawing

13 mm (½″)

Carcase side

Top carcase rail

Loose tongue

Corner post 25 mm (1″) sq.

Fig. 4b Plan View

the router jig. A dovetail cutter is used to cut the pins and tails in one operation, leaving the pins on the drawer front and tails on the drawer sides. Drawer guides are glued to the drawer runners but ensure the drawer is properly fitted before they are finally fixed. Drawer stops are fitted to the top of the bottom front rail.

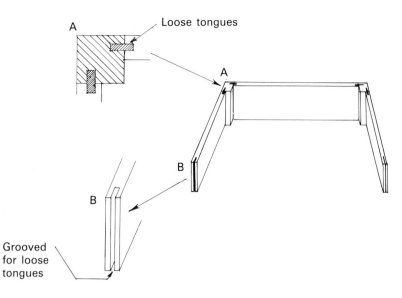

Step 1 Back and sides fitted into corner posts

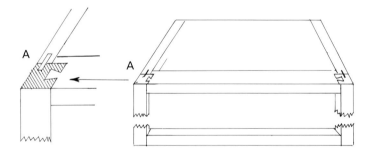

Step 2 With front drawer rails dovetailed

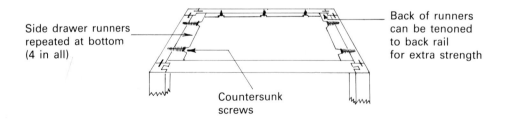

Step 3 Drawer runners are fitted and secured with two or three screws. Note backs of runners can be tenoned into the back rail for a more rigid assembly

Fig. 5 Carcase construction

84

Fig. 6 Machining the tenons on the router table

Fig. 7 Ready for grooving loose tongue

Legs and Brackets

Lap dovetails are used to join side stretchers onto the front and back legs, then brackets are shaped and fitted onto the leg posts and carcase base with loose tongue and grooves. Finally, legs are secured with screws through the stretchers to the carcase and the brackets are glued in. Suitable casters are fitted.

Clean up and sand the whole job thoroughly. Finish by french polishing in the traditional way for this period piece.

Note: The photograph (page 80) shows a slight variation for the top curved rail in the centre of the frame. If this design is preferred, the cutting list width of the rail should be adjusted for the extra shaping required.

Materials Cutting List

Item	No.	Length	Width	Thickness
Frame posts	4	250 mm $9\frac{7}{8}''$	25 mm $1''$	25 mm $1''$
Curved top frame rails	5*	484 mm $19''$	25 mm $1''$	13 mm $\frac{1}{2}''$
Bottom frame rails	5	484 mm $19''$	25 mm $1''$	13 mm $\frac{1}{2}''$
Middle frame rails	10	224 mm $8\frac{7}{8}''$	25 mm $1''$	13 mm $\frac{1}{2}''$
Side frame rails	6	224 mm $8\frac{7}{8}''$	13 mm $\frac{1}{2}''$	13 mm $\frac{1}{2}''$
Top and bottom side rails	4	231 mm $9''$	25 mm $1''$	13 mm $\frac{1}{2}''$
Side rails	6	224 mm $8\frac{7}{8}''$	25 mm $1''$	13 mm $\frac{1}{2}''$

Carcase sides	2	231mm 9″	100mm $3\frac{15}{16}$″	13mm $\frac{1}{2}$″
Carcase posts	4	100mm $3\frac{15}{16}$″	25mm 1″	25mm 1″
Carcase back	1	484mm 19″	100mm $3\frac{15}{16}$″	13mm $\frac{1}{2}$″
Carcase front rails	2	484mm 19″	50mm 2″	16mm $\frac{3}{8}$″
Frame bottom slats	4	484mm 19″	48mm $1\frac{7}{8}$″	13mm $\frac{1}{2}$″
Drawer runners	4	210mm $8\frac{1}{4}$″	30mm $1\frac{3}{16}$″	15mm $\frac{5}{8}$″
Drawer guides	2	210mm $8\frac{1}{4}$″	13mm $\frac{1}{2}$″	13mm $\frac{1}{2}$″
Drawer front	1	460mm 18″	70mm $2\frac{3}{4}$″	15mm $\frac{5}{8}$″
Drawer back	1	460 mm 18″	60mm $2\frac{3}{8}$″	13mm $\frac{1}{2}$″
Drawer sides	2	241mm $9\frac{1}{2}$″	13mm $\frac{1}{2}$″	70mm $2\frac{3}{4}$″
Drawer bottom plywood	1	444mm $17\frac{1}{2}$″	230mm $9\frac{1}{4}$″	4mm $\frac{3}{16}$″
Legs	4	160mm $6\frac{5}{16}$″	25mm 1″	25mm 1″
Side stretchers	2	233mm 9″	25mm 1″	15mm $\frac{5}{8}$″
Shaped brackets	4	120mm $4\frac{3}{4}$″	120mm $4\frac{3}{4}$″	13mm $\frac{1}{2}$″
Brass castors	4			
Brass drop handles	2			

*To be cut from 50mm(2″) width to allow for shaping

8. Tapestry Table in English Oak

Stan Hudson

DURING the many years I have spent designing and producing hand-made furniture much of my spare time has been occupied in browsing through churches and antique shops in order to examine and, hopefully, continue to learn from the best examples of woodwork from the past. Amongst much nondescript material may be found fine design and enviable execution which never fail to inspire me and I am sure many other dedicated woodworkers share this enthusiasm.

In the days when only very primitive and simple machines were available, handcrafts predominated, unlike today when sophisticated machines are everywhere in daily use, often, sadly, to the detriment of good design. It would seem that the high ratio of hand to machine techniques had much to do with the production of the finer pieces. Very difficult and delicate operations were carried out with skill and precision by craftsmen using only hand tools.

I suspect that these highly skilled artisans, and many not so skilled, deplored the preliminary mundane tasks such as sawing and chopping to size, and the removal of waste before the timber was ready for the more interesting final stages of trimming, jointing, fitting and finishing, involving the higher skills

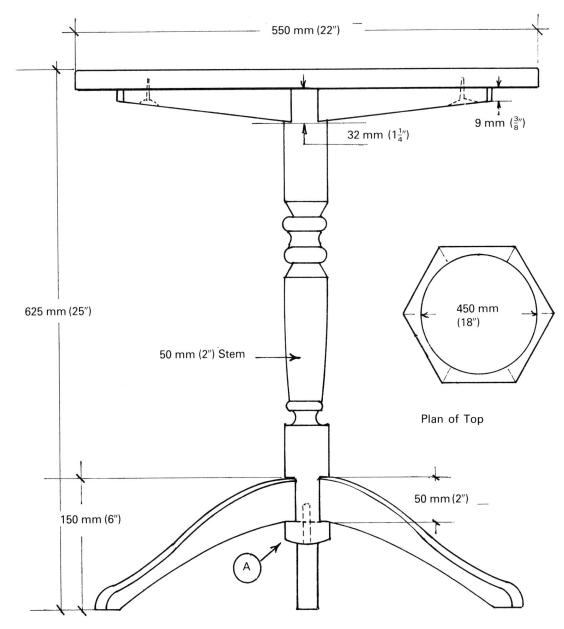

550 mm (22")

9 mm ($\frac{3}{8}$")

32 mm ($1\frac{1}{4}$")

625 mm (25")

450 mm (18")

50 mm (2") Stem

Plan of Top

50 mm (2")

150 mm (6")

A

Fig. 1 Side Elevation

which are the joy of all modern woodworkers.

The old craftsmen did of course avoid these unskilled chores by delegating them to the apprentice or labourer, a luxury we cannot afford today in many small or home workshops, but, thanks to technology, we do have many tools which can, properly used, reduce such work to a minimum.

One of the most efficient of these tools is the portable power router with its ability to remove

6 Off

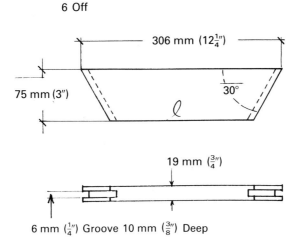

306 mm (12¼″)

75 mm (3″)

30°

ℓ

19 mm (¾″)

6 mm (¼″) Groove 10 mm (⅜″) Deep

Sizes shown are finished, ready
for assembly

Fig. 2 Section of top

waste very rapidly and accurately. With access-ories and attachments, and an almost infinite variety of cutter profiles, it has become an indispensable aid even to the near purist handworker.

I am regularly requested to mount hand-woven tapestries in such items as wall frames, firescreens and small tables, I have chosen a small tapestry table for this project as it is one of my popular repeat items and represents an attractive variation of a traditional design. Similar tables can be made from this design, for example, an octagonal top with four legs, a round or an oval top all with a tapestry, solid or veneered panel. Whatever the style the method of construction is the same with exten-sive use of the router in several stages of production.

Preparation of Individual Pieces

We begin by preparing all the separate items from the cutting list which gives finished dimensions. I have shown four pieces required for the legs although only three are needed for

the table but will explain this later. The next step is to shape the pieces as shown in the drawings. The stem is turned to a diameter of 50mm (2″) to any desired pattern and whilst in the lathe I mark with a pencil the top and bottom limits for the mortises right round the stem, ref. Fig. 1.

The template for the legs (Fig. 3) was cut in 4mm ply which allows the curves to be finished sweet and true with the spokeshave before transferring the shape to the leg timbers prior to bandsawing. It is only necessary to shape three, the fourth one being used only for setting and testing of the leg tenon on the router (Fig. 9i).

The six sections for the top frame must be finished exactly to the shape and size shown in Fig. 2 but without the grooves. The outside edge length must be identical on all six pieces and the angle must be 30 degrees, otherwise a true hexagon will not be developed on assembly. It is also essential to put a face mark on all pieces once the desired faces have been identified.

It only remains to finish the top supports to size as Fig. 3a.

89

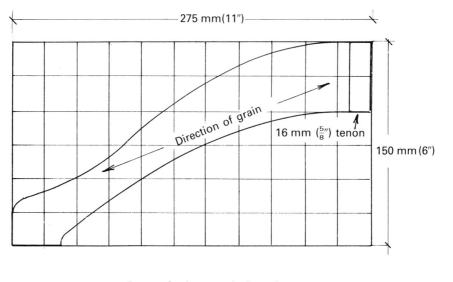

275 mm (11")

Direction of grain

16 mm ($\frac{5}{8}$") tenon

150 mm (6")

Pattern for legs marked out in
25 mm (1") squares

Fig. 3 Template for legs

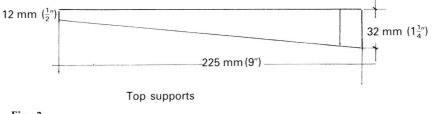

12 mm ($\frac{1}{2}$")

32 mm ($1\frac{1}{4}$")

225 mm (9")

Top supports

Fig. 3a

Cutting the Stem Joints

These are cut with the router using the very simple home-made jig shown in Fig. 7. Although made for repeats, it is simple and easy enough to make for a one-off. It is constructed with 19mm ($\frac{3}{4}$") thick beechwood and all the details are given in the drawing. The peg holes are spaced to give adequate control of the travel of the router in use. (I have been known, but never seen, to knock in the odd panel pin for this purpose but these are very private means to an end, invoking the Ways and Means Act.)

The stem must now be marked at both ends with the pin register lines on the same axis. Since my lathe has a dividing head, I mark these with a pencil at the required 120 degrees and transfer the marks to the end faces (Fig. 6). The details shown in Fig. 6 adequately explain the use and operation of the jig with the stem in position and the whole set-up held in the bench vice.

The first six cuts with the router, top and bottom, are made with two settings of the router fence and the depth of cut as at (A) Fig. 6, and the pin register lines set alternately against the pin. This cut produces the faces for the tenon shoulders. The second cut (B) Fig. 6 is the mortise cut on the centre line of the stem, again using the fence and rotating to the pin lines. In all these cuts the pass is left to right with complete control of the router achieved by ensuring the fence and base are in contact with the router base platform. Both cuts must take into account that the end of the mortise will be circular, and allowance must be made to square the joint with a chisel for the shoulders and the mortise proper. One finished joint is shown in Fig. 6. The stem is now finished and no more work on it is required except for final sanding.

Cutting and Assembly of Top Frame Sections

For mitre joints and small tenons I again use a home-made router table, details of which are shown in Fig. 8. This is constructed in 16mm ($\frac{5}{8}$″) beech. The top fence is separate and adjustable as indicated. The method of securing the router to the table depends of course on the make and type. My old Black and Decker H.D. which has done marathon service requires only three countersunk screws through the top face into the router baseplate.

Fig. 9 (2) shows the table held in the vice by the table extension A and used to groove the top sections. The fence is set so that the 6mm ($\frac{1}{4}$″) cutter is on the centre line of the top sections, a slight deviation here not being very important provided that the face marks of the sections are presented to the table for *all* cuts.

Check that the cutter extension 10mm ($\frac{3}{8}$″) is correct and pass the angled ends of all six sections across the cutter from left to right ensuring that the face side is in contact with the fence at all times. I find a rub with an old bit of candle on the fence makes for a nice smooth operation and helps prevent chatter. At each pass the ends must be in contact with the table face and the cut made positively and without hesitation in one confident movement. With all sections grooved they are now ready for assembly.

At this stage cut six oak "slips" 88mm ($3\frac{1}{2}$″) × 19mm ($\frac{3}{4}$″) less 1mm × 6mm ($\frac{1}{4}$″) *across the grain* on the 19mm ($\frac{3}{4}$″) face, so that on assembly the grain is continued from one section to the adjoining section across the groove. (The 1mm reduction in the 19mm ($\frac{3}{4}$″) dimension is to allow for the glue in the joint.) These slips at Fig. 4A may be trimmed to make a finger-push-fit

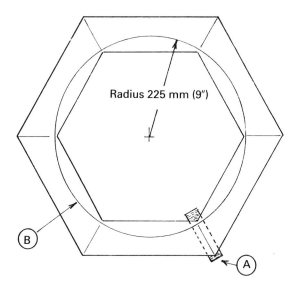

Assembled Top from Sections shown in Fig. 2.
A. Oak slips in grooved mitre joint.
B. Cutting line for inside edge of top marked on underside.

Fig. 4 Assembled top details

in the grooves. The crossgrain is shown in the drawing.

I use a piece of 19mm ($\frac{3}{4}$″) chipboard on which to assemble all mitred frames. After application of glue to the grooves the frames are placed together, one by one, with the slips in place to form the hexagon, making sure that all face side marks rest on the chipboard. Provided that the slips are not too tight, it is very easy to ensure that the joints match and close to finish the frame. Cramps are not required. Leave undisturbed for at least twenty-four hours. When dry, leave face down on the chipboard and secure with two cramps to prevent any movement.

From opposite mitre joint lines, mark the centre point on the chipboard and with a trammel scribe the 450mm (18″) circle on what is the underside of the top, checking that the line clears the inside corners of the frame. This

91

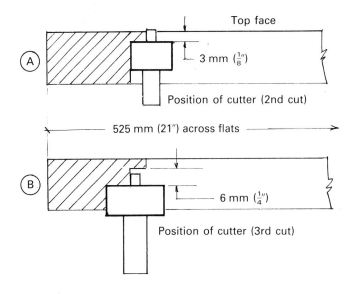

Top face

A
3 mm ($\frac{1}{8}$")

Position of cutter (2nd cut)

525 mm (21") across flats

B
6 mm ($\frac{1}{4}$")

Position of cutter (3rd cut)

A. Showing 2nd cut with 6 mm ($\frac{1}{4}$") Rebate Cutter with
   guide pin on inside circular edge of top
B. Showing a 3rd cut with 9 mm ($\frac{3}{8}$") Rebate Cutter in
   ($\frac{1}{4}$")rebate

Glass & Tapestry

9 mm ($\frac{3}{8}$") ply

Finished top

Fig. 5 Section through top rebates

circle is now cut with the jigsaw, following the line precisely, to leave a clean inside to the frame.

Since this top is to accommodate a glass-covered tapestry, the router is now used to cut the twin rebates; the method is shown in Fig. 5: two cuts to the depth of 16mm ($\frac{5}{8}$") for the first rebate A and one for the second rebate B which houses the 9mm ($\frac{3}{8}$") backboard, this being screwed to the frame as in the drawing.

When the frame has been cleaned up on the top face and sanded to a finish, the slips are planed off to match the corners before sanding the edges.

At this stage the top frame can be polished and the glass fitted, followed by the tapestry, mounted on a circle of 3mm ($\frac{1}{8}$") hardboard. The base backboard is screwed into position with 12mm ($\frac{1}{2}$") No. 6 screws.

Finishing the Legs and Top Supports

Check the three legs as cut from the template,

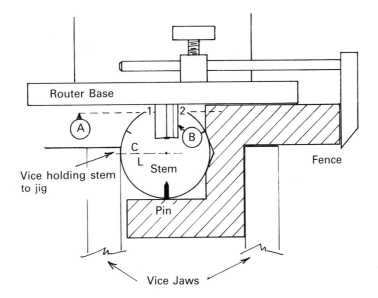

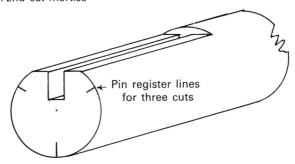

End elevation of Stem Joint Jig in vice with router set and adjusted to cutting the mortise and finished joint below top and bottom of stem
A. 1st cut shoulders 1 & 2 4 mm ($\frac{5}{32}$")
B. 2nd cut mortise

Fig. 6 Cutting stem joints

particularly the direction of grain, and ensure that the bottom face of the "foot" and the tenon face are square at 90 degrees. With the router mounted and the table in the upright position, it now operates as a miniature spindle moulder. Fig. 9 (1) shows the set-up and the adjustments to the fence and cutter height. Since the tenon needs to be a fairly tight push-fit in the open mortises, we must ensure the correct tenon thickness at the finish of the cuts. This is where the spare leg section is used and errors in adjustment corrected.

Take a first shallow cut across the end of the spare piece passing this time from right to left. Turn over and repeat. If necessary adjust the cutter height and repeat the cuts until the tenon fits the mortises. This sounds like a complicated operation but in fact takes only a few seconds and any errors are committed on the waste piece. When the fit is confirmed, and not too tight, the legs and top supports can be cut to completion.

Personally I like my tenons to be a fairly tight push-fit, and, always to this end, finally

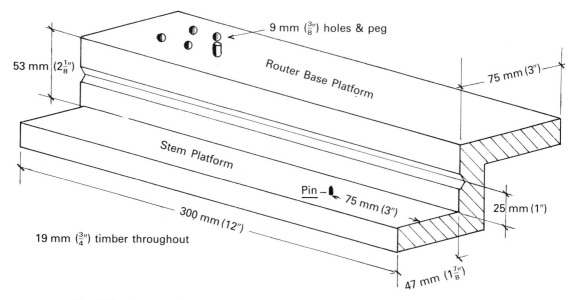

9 mm ($\frac{3}{8}''$) holes & peg

Router Base Platform

53 mm ($2\frac{1}{8}''$)

75 mm (3")

Stem Platform

Pin — 75 mm (3")

25 mm (1")

300 mm (12")

19 mm ($\frac{3}{4}''$) timber throughout

47 mm ($1\frac{7}{8}''$)

Fig. 7 Jig for stem joints

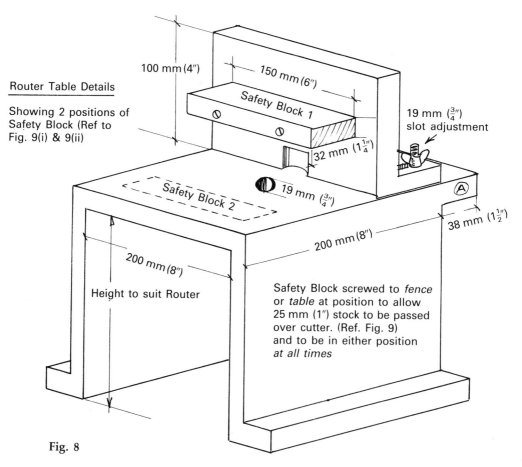

Router Table Details

Showing 2 positions of Safety Block (Ref to Fig. 9(i) & 9(ii))

100 mm (4")

150 mm (6")

Safety Block 1

19 mm ($\frac{3}{4}''$) slot adjustment

32 mm ($1\frac{1}{4}''$)

Safety Block 2

19 mm ($\frac{3}{4}''$)

Ⓐ

38 mm ($1\frac{1}{2}''$)

200 mm (8")

200 mm (8")

Height to suit Router

Safety Block screwed to *fence* or *table* at position to allow 25 mm (1") stock to be passed over cutter. (Ref. Fig. 9) and to be in either position *at all times*

Fig. 8

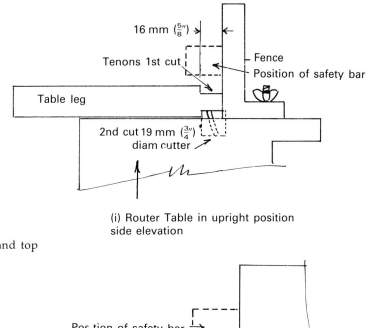

(i) Router Table in upright position
side elevation

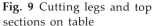

Fig. 9 Cutting legs and top
sections on table

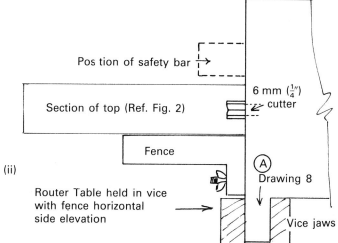

(ii)

fit by hand. Before I proceed to cut the tenons on the legs and supports, I place a piece of typewriter copy paper on the router table face, leaving fence and cutter as set for the test piece; the final passes are made over this paper which raises the timber, thus the tenon finishes slightly wider than the setting. This allows enough licence to trim and fit each joint, individually, with the shoulder plane.

The shoulders are left as cut, any very slight error here being of no consequence. It only remains to clean up all curves and faces to polishing stage. The top edges of the legs may be chamfered or rounded over using appropriate router cutters with guide pins. I glue and fit each leg separately and allow to dry. Final assembly of the table is as Fig. 1.

The bottom finial (A) in Fig. 1 is optional and was turned from scrap for the original and fixed with a centre dowel.

Safety First

A revolving cutter can reject a piece of timber offered to it in a fraction of a second leaving the fingers moving towards the cutter unprotected and reaction time nil. Do refer to Figs. 8 and 9 in this project and ensure that safety blocks are fixed in position before passing any pieces over the revolving cutters.

95

Cutting List

Item	No.	Length	Width	Thickness
Stem	1	500 mm 20″	54 mm $2\frac{1}{8}″$	54 mm $2\frac{1}{8}″$
Legs	4*	325 mm 13″	75 mm 3″	22 mm $\frac{7}{8}″$
Top supports	3	225 mm 9″	32 mm $1\frac{1}{4}″$	22 mm $\frac{7}{8}″$
Top sections	6	306 mm $12\frac{1}{4}″$	75 mm 3″	22 mm $\frac{7}{8}″$
Ply back for top (underside)	1	482 mm $19\frac{1}{4}″$ dia.		9 mm $\frac{3}{8}″$
Cross grain slips	6	To size in text. Allow for trimming to fit.		

*Only three legs required for cutting to template. Fourth used for setting router cutter for leg tenons. This piece need not necessarily be the size as quoted above but must be finished from the leg material at 22 mm ($\frac{7}{8}″$).

9. Decorated Bowl

Michael O'Donnell

The Router & the Lathe

Using a rotating cutter in conjunction with the lathe is nothing new. It has been done for hundreds of years and, indeed, is the method of cutting used with ornamental turning. The big difference in using a router with the lathe is that the cutter has its own motor, independent of the lathe motor. The advantage of this is that the need for a complicated drive belt linkage is eliminated and the router can be used on a conventional woodturning lathe with some simple additions to its normal function:

a) A method of indexing the lathe spindle

which can be altered to suit any particular situation.

b) A method of locking the lathe spindle at each of the indexing points.

c) A method of fixing the router securely to the lathe.

d) A method of precisely controlling the position and direction of movement of the cutter.

I see the router used on the lathe as a method of adding decoration or texture to the surface of a previously turned piece, rather than making the whole project with the router.

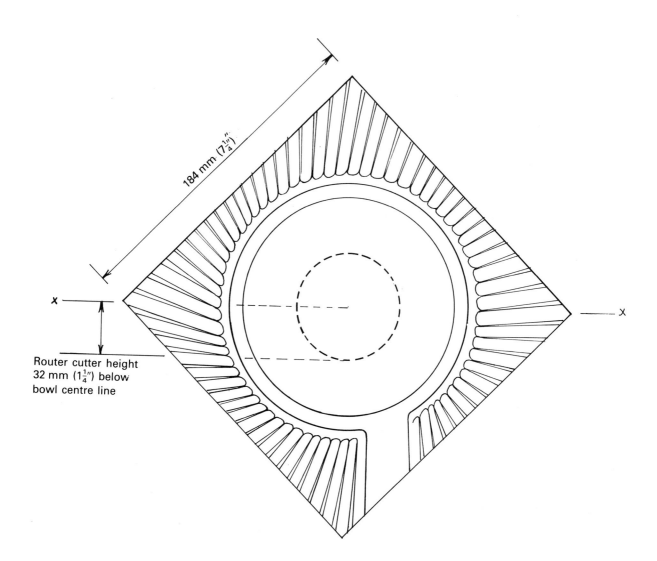

184 mm (7¼")

x

Router cutter height
32 mm (1¼") below
bowl centre line

X

Section on X.X.

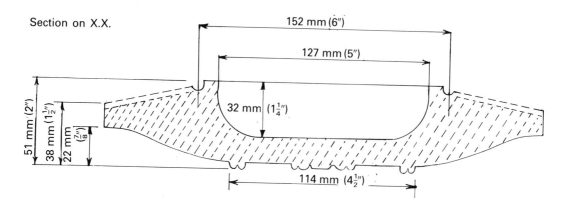

152 mm (6")

127 mm (5")

32 mm (1¼")

51 mm (2")

38 mm (1½")

22 mm (⅞")

114 mm (4½")

98

The Project

With this project, as with many others, the most important aspect is the *planning*, and here the surface decoration plays a very important part. There can be a lot of problems associated with using the router on the lathe, so for a first attempt it is a good idea to keep the project simple; for mine, I have chosen to decorate the rim of a bowl.

If we use a narrow rim then the overall effect on the bowl is going to be minimal therefore a wide rim would be a more effective surface.

I decided on a small chunky bowl but felt that being round wasn't going to be interesting enough, so I made it square.

Turning a square bowl can be difficult but is not impossible. There are three methods depending on what you feel happiest with:

1) Turn the piece square but watch your fingers and be careful about breakaway on the edges.
2) Turn a solid round piece then cut it square when completed.
3) Glue on soft woodwaste blocks to the sides of the square piece to make it round for turning, then cut them off when completed. (This is a method perfected by Vic Wood of Australia.)

I would recommend methods 2 or 3.

I don't think there is any point in going to any elaborate and costly jig arrangements for the router unless you plan to do a lot of routering or production runs. The following methods are cheap, quick and easy to make up with minimal equipment. Elaborate on them after, if you wish.

Holding the router is the first problem to tackle. If it is mounted horizontally it will be in a position to work across the rim of a bowl or axially along a spindle if required. My router, an Elu Electronic variable speed, is supplied with two bars as part of the guide system. If we fix these into the base, then turn the router so that they are vertical, we can see that if the bottom ends of the bars were fixed into a block then this would be a satisfactory holding method and one which also gives us some

control over the cutter height. We also need a surface for the block to stand and move about on and a piece of ply clamped to the lathe bed will serve this purpose.

Methods of controlling the movement will depend upon the type of movement required. For this bowl, a simple straight line is all that is wanted and a guide bar clamped to the ply will provide a guide for the router base block to slide against. Now that alone would be fine if we were to come in at one side of the rim and out at the other. As we are not, then a stop for the end of the cut will make the job much easier.

The indexing can be achieved by fixing a large face plate or piece of ply to the outboard spindle which can be marked out in increments around the edge. The larger the disc, the easier it is to mark out and the more accurate to use. Some form of pointer is required to line up the marks.

Fig. 1 Elu router mounted in stand

99

Fig. 2 Guide bar and stop for router movement

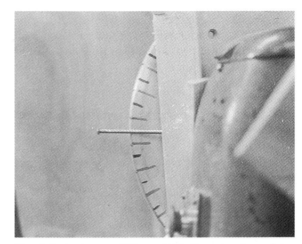

Fig. 3 Indexing on 356mm (14″) diameter face plate

Rather than lock the spindle in each position, I opted for a friction brake, which held the spindle securely enough, but not so tight that I couldn't turn the index plate with one hand. A nail in the brake arm provided a pointer for the indexing.

Now that we have the basic set-up, we need to arrange the jig and router for this particular job. If the cutter is set at the lathe axis height then the grooves will all be radial. By raising or lowering the cutter the grooves then become tangential to increasing diameter circles and look more interesting. Set the cutter as low as possible which is 32mm (1¼″) below the axis, then set the guide bar parallel to the rim at this point. To do this, hold a straight edge horizontally against the rim at the cutter height then look vertically down on it and line up the guide. This isn't necessarily the correct position to give the depth of cut required, but it is at the right angle, so draw a line on the base

board along the guide to record this direction. Use a 6mm (¼″) diameter half round cutter and set the plunge to about 10mm (⅜″) less than maximum depth. Put the router on the base so that the cutter is touching the rim, with the front edge of the stand parallel to the line drawn on the base, then bring the guide bar up against it. The depth of cut can be set by either fixing the guide bar in this position and adjusting the depth of plunge, or moving the guide bar back by the required depth, fixing it and making fine corrections with the plunger depth. We also need a stop for the end of the cut, so, line up the router cutter at the required point and clamp on a stop bar, touching the side of it.

The last part of the setting up is to decide on the increments at which we require the grooves. I wanted a space between the grooves at the outer edge and then for them to overlap as they come closer to the centre.

Maximum outer diameter 267mm (10½″) circumference = π(3.142) × dia = 839mm (33″)
Inner diameter 152mm (6″) circumference = π × dia = 478mm (18.85″)

If we arrange that the grooves just touch at 152mm (6″) diameter the number of increments would be 478 ÷ 6.35 = 75 (18.85″ ÷ 1/4″ = 75) I rounded that down to 72 because my index plate was already marked at that, the difference it makes would be negligible.

At the outer limits there will be 5mm ($\frac{3}{16}$″) between grooves. (The cutter will make a 6mm ($\frac{1}{4}$″) wide groove with a 3mm ($\frac{1}{8}$″) depth of cut.)

The outer rim of the index plate should now be divided into 76 (or 72) increments.

For the brake I clamped a piece of 50 × 25mm (2″ × 1″) to the bed for a brake arm, then placed a wedge between the headstock and the arm so that the arm pressed against the index plate, tapping the wedge in, to give the required braking effect. Drive a long nail into the brake arm as a marker for the indexing. (Fig. 3).

Because from this stage you will not be using the power on the lathe, reaching for the lathe switch by mistake could cause an accident so unplug it and wear ear muffs as protection against the router noise.

To make the first cut, line up one of the index marks with the pointer; then line up the router along the guide with the cutter just outside the outer edge of the bowl and switch on the router. Take a firm hold of the base then push it firmly along the guide to the stop, then take it out of the cut and return it to the start position. For the second cut move the index plate to the next mark and repeat. You don't need to be too accurate in positioning the index mark as a small element of irregularity in the position of the grooves improves its appeal.

As with turning, we can run into end grain problems on certain sections. Making some of the cuts from the centre to the rim will help in such circumstances. Watch the quality of the cuts as you go. (Figs. 4 and 7).

With my bowl, I planned to leave a section

Fig. 4 Positioning the router to take a cut

Fig. 5 Detail of finished bowl

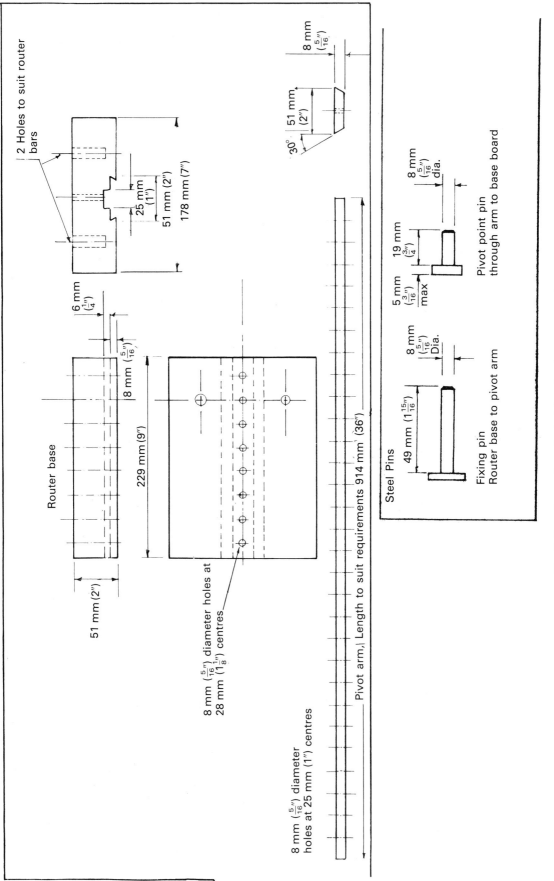

2 Holes to suit router bars

8 mm ($\frac{5''}{16}$)

51 mm (2")

30°

25 mm (1")

51 mm (2")

178 mm (7")

6 mm ($\frac{1''}{4}$)

8 mm ($\frac{5''}{16}$)

Router base

229 mm (9")

51 mm (2")

8 mm ($\frac{5''}{16}$) diameter holes at 28 mm ($1\frac{1''}{8}$) centres

8 mm ($\frac{5''}{16}$) diameter holes at 25 mm (1") centres

Pivot arm, Length to suit requirements 914 mm (36")

Steel Pins

8 mm ($\frac{5''}{16}$) dia.

19 mm ($\frac{3''}{4}$)

5 mm ($\frac{3''}{16}$) max

Pivot point pin through arm to base board

8 mm ($\frac{5''}{16}$) Dia.

49 mm ($1\frac{15''}{16}$)

Fixing pin Router base to pivot arm

Fig. 6 Base for router adapted for circular movement

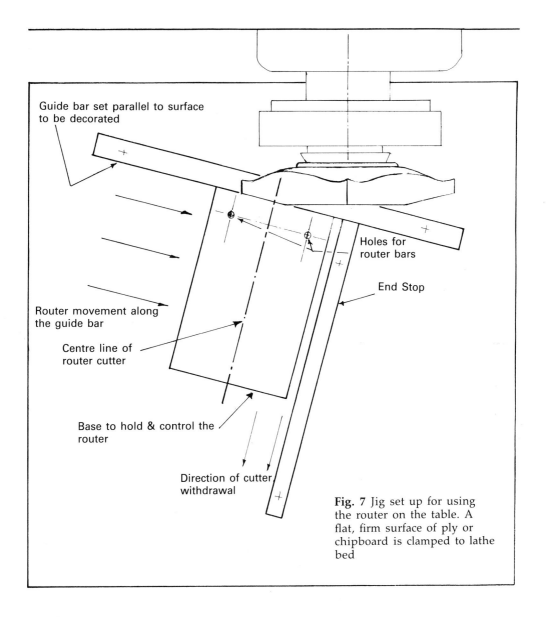

Guide bar set parallel to surface to be decorated

Holes for router bars

End Stop

Router movement along the guide bar

Centre line of router cutter

Base to hold & control the router

Direction of cutter withdrawal

Fig. 7 Jig set up for using the router on the table. A flat, firm surface of ply or chipboard is clamped to lathe bed

without grooves but had not decided how much. It was just a matter of taking cuts until it looked right.

The ends of the cuts may need a little tidying up all the way round, and if so you can increase the depth of cut a little by adjusting the router plunger, pushing the base along the end stop till it reaches the guide, hold it there firmly and rotate the spindle by hand.

Some edges may need a little sanding, but apart from that the machining is complete.

I finished my project with three coats of Danish oil. The result is a very pleasant chunky little bowl which is nice to handle.

If the surface to be decorated is circular then a further modification to the jig is necessary and is detailed in Fig. 6.

10. Chinese Chequers Board

Simon Thorne

THE game of Chinese chequers has been played throughout the centuries and is still very popular today. The chequers board traditionally comprises a star shape, the six points of which house each player's ten "men". The aim is for each player to move all ten men into the opposite player's home area. Counters or marbles can progress by jumping over other counters or by moving one space in any direction. At no time are any pieces removed from the board; the winner is the first to position all ten men in the opponent's home. The game can be enjoyed by 2 to 6 players.

The beauty of this project is that it can be made to whatever size you require, depending on your preference or the availability of suitable marbles to be used as counters.

The following is a list of requirements:

1) Power hand router with plunge action, capable of taking a collar.
2) 9mm ($\frac{3}{8}$") tungsten carbide tipped nosing cutter and moulding cutter (optional).
3) 370 × 370 × 9mm (14 $\frac{1}{2}$" × 14 $\frac{1}{2}$" × $\frac{3}{8}$") plywood for the jig.
4) 4 off. 200 × 25 × 25mm (8" × 1" × 1") locating blocks, fixed with 30mm (1 $\frac{1}{4}$") No. 6 countersunk screws.

5) 320 × 320 × 25mm (12 ½″ × 12 ½″ × 1″) African mahogany for the board; other timbers are equally suitable.

The most difficult part of this project is probably the geometry of the jig hole centres. The plywood jig should be cut accurately to a 370mm (14½″) square and the centre of the square located. Whenever accurate jig work is being set out it is advisable to use a hard pencil, for example a 2H, as it keeps its point and remains accurate. The hole centres should be marked out from the centre of the ply jig, the procedure is as follows:

1) draw a 140mm (5½″) radius circle.

2) using the circle to determine where the points of the star will occur, draw an equilateral triangle, pointing along the grain of the board inside the circle.
3) Turn the board around and draw a similar triangle. You should now have a six-sided star, a "Star of David".
4) Mark in all the lines as shown in the main drawing to obtain the remainder of the hole centres.

It should be stressed at this stage how important the accuracy of the setting out is. Poor setting out causes inaccuracies which are very difficult to rectify later on.

Most modern, powered, hand routers are

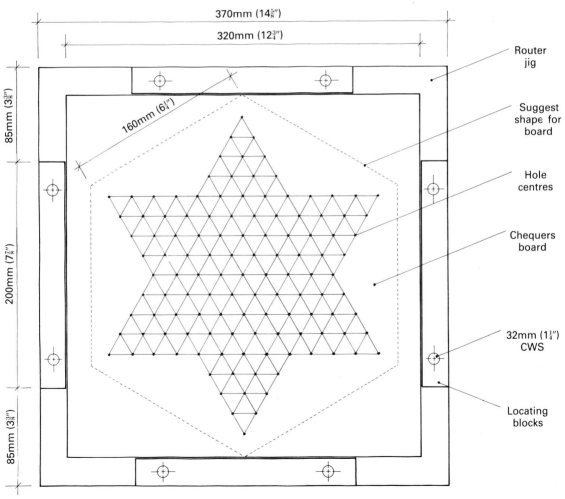

105

designed with a plunge action and come complete with a collar. If your router does not have a collar, one can be obtained from a main stockist. (The collar is incorporated in a plate which is fixed into a recess on the sole of the router.)

Having determined the size of the collar (a 15mm ($\frac{5}{8}$") collar was used in this instance) holes should be carefully drilled through the pre-marked centres on the plywood jig. It is a good idea to use either a twist drill with a point ground on it or a high speed flat bit which also has a point. The importance of the point is to prevent the drill from skidding across the board. Using a pillar drill will greatly help the vertical alignment of the holes. All the holes having been drilled it is a good idea to lightly sand both sides of the jig to remove any protruding woolly fibres or splinters.

(Plywood is very prone to break out or splinter on the back when being drilled. To help prevent this, a scrap board should be cramped to the back of the ply.)

The pre-cut chequers board should be carefully placed in the centre of the jig and the locating blocks glued and screwed in place round the four sides of the board. The jig and the board are now ready for routing.

The router should be set up to allow the cutter to protrude sufficiently below the jig in order to produce suitably sized holes for the marbles you have chosen. Set the depth stop to allow this adjustment to be made. Before starting on your board it is a good idea to rout a test scrap-piece first just to check that everything is working as it should and that you are taking the right amount of cut.

The holes should now be routed. The router should be plunged in and out quickly as there is a tendency for the cutter to burn the wood if left down too long.

Having completed the holes, the board can

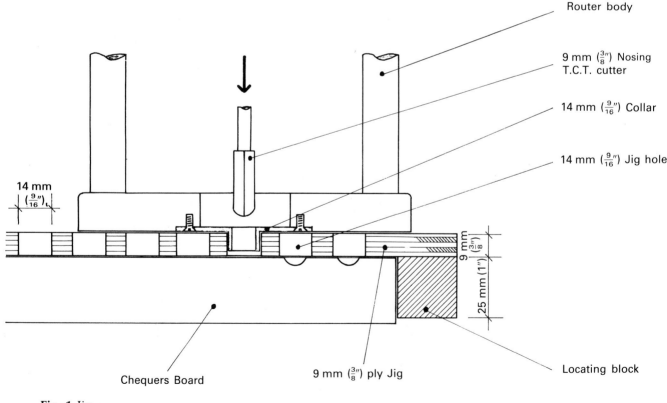

Router body

9 mm ($\frac{3}{8}$") Nosing T.C.T. cutter

14 mm ($\frac{9}{16}$") Collar

14 mm ($\frac{9}{16}$") Jig hole

14 mm ($\frac{9}{16}$")

9 mm ($\frac{3}{8}$")

25 mm (1")

Chequers Board

9 mm ($\frac{3}{8}$") ply Jig

Locating block

Fig. 1 Jig

Fig. 2 The plywood jig drilled to pattern

Fig. 3 The router plunges through the jig

either be left square, or cut into a hexagonal shape, or a circle, depending on choice. It looks better with some form of moulding around the edge. The moulding on the sample was done with the same nosing cutter used for the holes together with a router fence. However, it would be easier to use one of the readily available moulding cutters.

The board can be finished to your own requirements. This board was sanded down to a 250 grit. It was then stained with a mahogany stain and lacquered. The ten holes in each point of the star should have their own colour, corresponding with that of the marbles you choose. This can be done with an eye dropper using model enamel paints, but it is important that you put the paint in the holes after the board has been lacquered otherwise the paint has a tendency to creep along the grain of the wood.

This project is very quick, and as long as the jig is well made it is very simple to do. The sizes can be altered easily to suit your own needs which makes it an ideal project for small batch production for articles to sell at craft fairs, or as Christmas gifts, etc.

Fig. 4 The chequers board routed through and ready for shaping and moulding

108

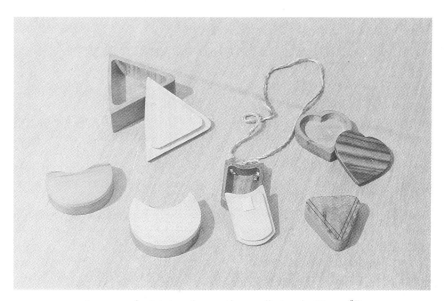

A group of miniature boxes, the smallest only 19mm ($\frac{3}{4}''$) maximum dimension. One has been strung as a locket and has a small pad of chamois leather to maintain the tight fit of the lid

11. Miniature Loose-lidded Boxes

Richard Windley

THIS project describes the making of small loose-lidded boxes of various shapes routed from solid wood and utilises a router fitted with a template guide (this is a round metal washer with a shallow projecting flange which screws to the underside of the router base) plus simple plywood templates.

The first job is to make the two templates required, one for routing the recessed base and one for the lip of the lid. It should be noted that the accuracy of the finished work, particularly the close fitting of the lids, depends on the marking-out and cutting of the templates. If batch production, to which these techniques

are well suited, is intended, fastidious workmanship will be amply repaid.

The dimension of the templates will depend on the final size of the box, the radius of the template ring guide (which should be as small as possible) and the diameter of the cutter employed. For small boxes, particularly those having acute internal corners, the smallest available parallel flute cutter may be used with advantage.

Start by marking out the shape required directly onto 6mm ($\frac{1}{4}''$) plywood which should be about 200 × 150mm (8″ × 6″) for boxes up to about 50mm (2″) maximum dimension. This

109

outline should then be enlarged by: (template guide diameter minus cutter diameter) $\times \frac{1}{2}$. When this is satisfactorily marked out, carefully cut out the centre with a fretsaw or coping saw, cutting as close to the *inside* of the marked line as possible. Clean up the edges and sand to a reasonable finish. This will be the template for the routed box-base.

Mark the upper surface "TOP" then invert; place over the second piece of ply and draw with a sharp pencil around the cut-out. Remove this first template and enlarge the marked outline on the second piece by the exact diameter of the router cutter to be used. It is advisable to measure with callipers; if the cutter has been sharpened regularly it may have become smaller than its nominal size. Remove the centre by sawing, as before, but this time cut just to the outside of the line. Mark "Top" or "Upper" to avoid accidental inversion and clean up the edges with sandpaper. This will be the lid template.

When this has been done, screw two parallel battens about 25 × 25mm (1″ × 1″) to each ply template with countersunk screws. These should be spaced about 6mm ($\frac{1}{4}$″) past each extreme edge of the outline (see Fig. 1). Cut and dress the workpieces from which the bases are to be machined until the wood is a snug sliding fit in the first (box-base) jig. The thickness of this wood should be about 19mm

($\frac{3}{4}$″) for small boxes up to say 50mm (2″) largest dimension. This gives a reasonable proportion to the finished box; if it is thicker, it can give a rather heavy, ponderous appearance which is not so pleasing. If a length of wood of about 450–500mm (18″–20″) is used it helps to speed up production; up to eight or nine mini-boxes can be quickly routed and the whole set-up will still be quite manageable.

As far as choice of timbers is concerned, any reasonably dense and easily machined wood should work well. I have used luan, iroko, afrormosia and opepe successfully. However, for a first trial it is prudent to use off-cuts of any hardwood which may be to hand to avoid wastage if the templates are not accurate. In this case, they must be re-made until correct. A certain amount of trial-and-error is inevitable until a little experience is gained in cutting them out.

Clamp the workpiece and the jig in a bench-vice making sure the workpiece is firmly "pinched" by the sides of the jig and that the top of the workpiece is in contact with the underside of the template. Rub a little candle-wax around the edge of the template to help the ring-guide slide and the routing can commence.

Set the maximum depth on the depth stop, this will be in the order of 14mm ($\frac{9}{16}$″) with 19mm ($\frac{3}{4}$″) workpiece, then place router template guide inside template and hold it firmly against

Fig. 1 The completed box base jig, workpiece and one routed base recess

Fig. 2 The completed lid jig together with workpiece and backing block, showing one routed lid blank

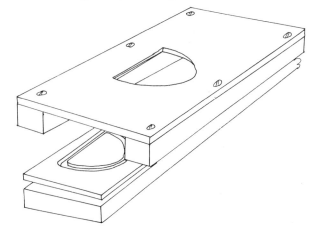

one edge. Switch on router and take a shallow cut around the periphery in a clockwise direction then back and forth to remove the "island" of wood in the middle. Repeat this procedure almost to maximum depth and take a final very shallow cut with the router moved slowly around to give as good a finish as possible of the base of the recess as this is very difficult to sand at a later stage.

Switch off router, remove jig from vice, move wood along to give about 12mm ($\frac{1}{2}$") between recesses and repeat the whole procedure until all the number of bases have been routed. (See Fig. 1)

We now proceed to the second "lid" jig. The timber for the lids need not necessarily be the same as their corresponding bases. I prefer to use expensive exotics and special pieces for the lids and use more easily obtainable and sometimes stabler woods for the bases. This can also give interesting colour combinations.

The thickness of the solids need only be about 4.5mm ($\frac{3}{16}$") so a backing piece about 19mm ($\frac{3}{4}$") will be helpful to keep it in position in the jig. Clamp the two pieces in the jig in the bench vice and check particularly that the workpiece is held firmly, as any subsequent movement will result in a wasted lid. Place router with template guide inside template, hold tightly against the edge and switch on. Take a shallow cut of about 2mm ($\frac{3}{32}$") around

the periphery. It is absolutely vital that the template guide is held firmly against the edge of the template as any tendency to move towards the centre will again result in a wasted lid. This is the trickiest part of the proceedings but with care should not present too much difficulty. Repeat the procedure, moving the workpiece along and leaving a space of about 6mm ($\frac{1}{4}$") between adjacent lids until as many lids as required have been routed. (See Fig. 2)

This completes the routing operation.

The box outline can now be marked out on the workpiece with a simple marking gauge made from a thin stick and pencil taped together. Ideally the spacing should give a line about 3mm ($\frac{1}{8}$") from the edge. (See Fig. 3) The boxes should then be sawn out on a band-saw or fret-saw just outside the marked line and finished by sanding either by hand which is very tedious or by sanding discs down to about 320 grit.

The lids can be marked in a similar way, but from the inner "step" 3mm ($\frac{1}{8}$") outwards, sawn-out and placed on a sanded box and brought down to the same profile by sanding. (Fig. 4) It often happens that with internal angles anomalies occur due to the radius of the router cutter. In these cases it is necessary to pare a little off the offending corner projections of the lid lip with a sharp chisel until a satisfactory fit is obtained. This is why the smallest router

Fig. 3 The simple marking gauge for drawing the finished box outline

Fig. 4 The form of a completed box showing recessed lip on box lid

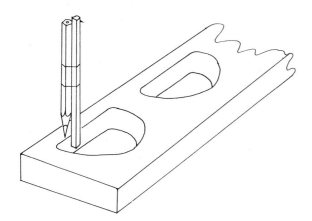

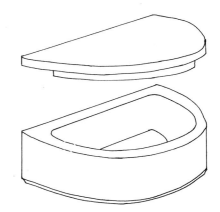

cutter available was suggested earlier in the project.

Finally, the boxes can be finished by hand, using 400 grit paper followed by sanding sealer, 0000 wire wool and Briwax.

When the lids are made of strongly coloured or figured woods, they will probably look interesting and attractive without further embellishment. However, when using more bland timbers such as sycamore or even the less strongly marked satinwoods etc., a simple resin line-inlay technique may be used to good effect. This works particularly well with the more geometric shapes and can give a nice "frame" effect when used parallel to the edges. Cross-hatching to produce a series of diamond shapes can also be very effective. The secret, like ornamental turning, is to apply the decorative effect sparingly and not get carried-away with the technique to the detriment of the finished object.

The technique is quite simple: mark-out the desired pattern carefully in pencil, then fix the lid so that it is firm; with a straight-edge as a guide, saw a fine line with a very fine brass-back saw, to a depth of about 1.5mm ($\frac{1}{16}$"). I use the saw blade from an X-acto Knife Set, which is available separately from model shops. Rub off any roughness with the edge of a piece of fine sandpaper, apply a coat of sealer to the lid, particularly the edges of the saw-cuts, and when dry, run the saw through to clean-up and give another rub with the sandpaper. This helps to stop the glue from being absorbed by the wood and leaving an unsightly bleed mark.

Next, mix the resin (one of the 5-minute twin-pack epoxys seems to work quite well) and when well mixed, add just a little children's powder paint and mix again. Apply the resin to the saw-cuts, working it well into the grooves; run a sharp tool along to make sure that the resin is smoothly down, especially at the ends which are visible. Use more resin than is needed, to allow for shrinkage and to lessen the chances of air-bubbles appearing, then set aside to dry. It is advisable to make-up a trial mixture before using it on a lid as sometimes a chemical reaction between pigment and glue stops it setting properly. In this case a little trial-and-error is required, with different pigments, until satisfactory results are obtained. When the glue appears to be fully set, sand off the excess with progressively finer discs and finish as for the boxes.

Cabinet in African walnut, using a linseed oil finish

12. Wall-hung Cabinet in Solid Hardwood

Peter Kuh

This cabinet is made from hardwood using basic methods of solid timber construction, cutting a number of traditional joints using your router. You should end up with a handsome and useful piece of furniture which has cost relatively little to make.

I recommend using one of the less expensive, more stable timbers such as beech, chestnut or sycamore. If you have more to spend you could use oak or an imported timber such as Brazilian mahogany. Make sure that the timber is sufficiently dry (around 14% moisture content if kiln-dried and no more than 18% if air-dried) and be sure to make an adequate allowance for waste.

Prepare the timber to the exact sizes given on the cutting list, but, don't forget, solid timber will always react to changes around it (humidity, temperature or machining) so once it has been prepared, keep the pieces flat by cramping them to a flat surface or keeping heavy weights on them.

To make the carcase, start by marking out all the joints on the sides, top and bottom. First, cut the grooves for the 6mm ($\frac{1}{4}''$) ply back on the inside of each part of the carcase 6mm ($\frac{1}{4}''$) in from the back edge. This groove is 6mm ($\frac{1}{4}''$) deep and runs right through on the sides but is stopped on the top and bottom 11mm ($\frac{7}{16}''$) in from each end. Make sure that your plywood

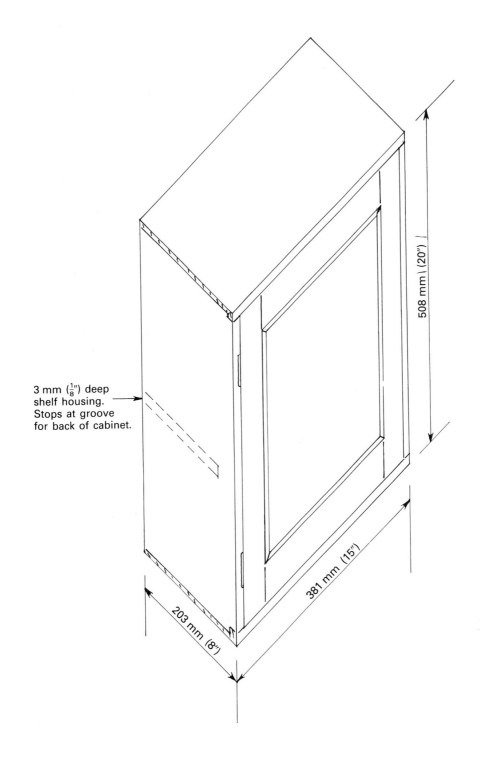

3 mm ($\frac{1}{8}''$) deep
shelf housing.
Stops at groove
for back of cabinet.

508 mm (20″)

381 mm (15″)

203 mm (8″)

114

fits in the groove; if you use birch plywood it may be necessary to increase the width of the groove slightly.

Next, cut the corner joints as shown in the photographs. When setting up the router to make the joint, try each cut first on an off-cut. Once all the cuts have been made you can fit one piece of off-cut to another to avoid any possible damage to the pieces of the cabinet itself. Make sure that the tongue doesn't fit too tightly in the groove; if it does the short grain of the tongue will break off when the joint is fitted. Note that the depth of the groove on the top and bottom is exactly the same as the depth of the groove in the endgrain on the sides; keep one of the depth-stops on your router for this depth of cut. Since the joint is stopped at the front, run the cuts right through on the sides, but stop the cuts 6mm ($\frac{1}{4}$") in from the front edge on the top and bottom. With a sharp

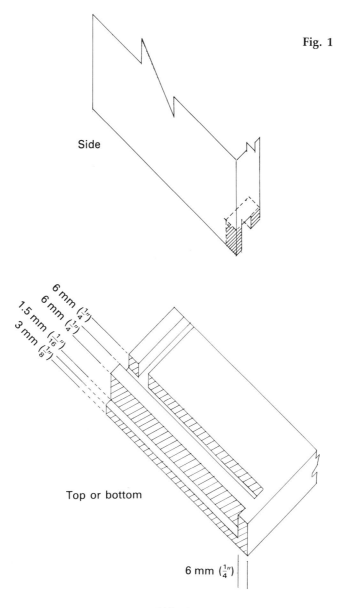

Fig. 1

Side

6 mm ($\frac{1}{4}$")
6 mm ($\frac{1}{4}$")
1.5 mm ($\frac{1}{16}$")
3 mm ($\frac{1}{8}$")

Top or bottom

6 mm ($\frac{1}{4}$")

Fig. 2 First cut in top and bottom corner joint; 6mm ($\frac{1}{4}''$) groove stopped at front

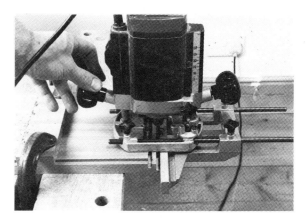

Fig. 3 Second cut in top and bottom corner; 12mm ($\frac{1}{2}''$) deep rebate made in two depths of cut (fence setting remains constant)

chisel accurately square up the small amount of remaining waste. If you are not very experienced with your router it would be wise to fix a clear perspex sub-base for making these corner joints, otherwise, when making the grooves in the endgrain of the sides, the cutter plunges in too deeply when you come near to the edge and you only have half of the router base bearing on the endgrain. As an alternative, mount the router in a router table, then cut the grooves.

The final joint in the carcase is the stopped housing for a shelf. This must house the full thickness of the shelf very snugly since any sloppiness in the joint will be seen above or below the shelf. When you fit the shelf be careful when you remove it from the housing, since it will want to take small chips out of the endgrain of the housing. This can be avoided by clamping battens along each side of the housing before removing the shelf. Remember to stop the housing 38mm ($1\frac{1}{2}''$) in from the front edge. This allows for the door to close in front of the shelf and for 6mm ($\frac{1}{4}''$) shoulders to be cut on the front corners of the shelf which will conceal the front of the housing.

Once you are sure that all pieces will fit (including the ply back which should be 3mm ($\frac{1}{8}''$) shorter and narrower than the full length and width of its groove) clean up all the interior surfaces of each piece. Do this with a scraper

and successive grades of garnet paper (say 80, 120, 150 and 180 grit) making sure that each finer grade removes all scratches left by the previous grade. Take care on the ends of the sides and the shelf; if you sand too much away you will be left with a sloppy joint.

Prepare all blocks and sash cramps before gluing up. Start by gluing the shelf into the housing, fit the ply back between the sides (no glue necessary here) then glue the corner joints. It is *very important* to locate the sides with the top and bottom accurately the first time; once they are fitted together you might ruin the joint if you try to separate them. Measure the diagonals of the carcase to make sure it is square. Using blocks and sash cramps as shown, leave the glue to set (at least 6 hours if using PVA glue). Sight along the sides and top and bottom to make sure none are bowing out; if they are, adjustment of the cramps or a tap with a block and hammer will usually solve the problem.

Once the glue has set, clean up the projecting endgrain with a finely adjusted sharp block plane. Then clean up the outside of the carcase with a scraper and garnet paper.

To make the door you must first decide whether you will glaze it or use a solid panel. You can also use the cabinet in the bathroom and put a mirror in the door.

If the frame is to be glazed, a rebate for the

glass will run round the inside of the door; the frame is jointed with mortise and tenon joints with long and short shoulders.

If the frame is to have a solid panel, a 6mm ($\frac{1}{4}''$) groove runs around the inside edge right through each piece. The grooves on the ends of the stiles are filled with the haunches on the tenons. (Note: haunches have not been used on the tenons shown in the photos.)

To cut the mortises, set the depth stop for just over 25mm (1") deep cut and using a long 6mm ($\frac{1}{4}''$) cutter, make a series of plunging cuts to the full depth. Then remove the waste between the holes with more plunging cuts and finally make one cut to the full depth along the length of the mortise. Square up the ends of the mortise with a 6mm ($\frac{1}{4}''$) chisel.

To cut the tenons it is best to use a router

Fig. 4 First cut in sides' corner joint; 12mm ($\frac{1}{2}''$) deep 6mm ($\frac{1}{4}''$) in from inside fence. Cut goes right through

Fig. 5 Second cut in sides' corner. This reduces the length of the tongue to 6mm ($\frac{1}{4}''$)

Fig. 6 Completed joint after squaring up front shoulders accurately with a chisel

Fig. 7 Corner joint fitted dry. It should be a hand-tight fit after inside surfaces have been cleaned up

Fig. 8 Gluing-up carcase. Ensure that sash cramps stand far enough from the sides to allow location of blocks for cramping the shelf. These cramps should run parallel to the sides. Make sure that none of the sash cramps bow the sides or the top and bottom

Fig. 9 Door construction. Door panel has been cleaned up. Door is ready for gluing

table and mitre-gauge.

Make a series of passes over the cutter on each side of the tenon. The tenons should be a snug, hand-tight fit in the mortises and the face sides should line up accurately with each other. The key to doing good work with your router is to use sharp cutters and never to take too deep a cut; the more strain there is on the router, the less control you will have over it.

To make a solid panel, either use one width of solid timber (be careful of cupping, which is likely unless the timber is quarter-sawn) or butt-joint two pieces, preferably book-matched. The panel should be about 3mm ($\frac{1}{8}$″) shorter and narrower than the size of the groove cut for it. Rout the moulding detail of your choice around the front edge of the panel. Usually this will involve a rebate around the outside which reduces the thickness of the panel to the width of the groove and a shaped cut to give a smooth transition from the surface of the panel to the rebate. After cleaning up the mouldings and panel (front and back) the panel should be a snug hand-tight fit in the groove. Don't force it, you might split the groove! Polish the panel before gluing up the door. Locate the panel in

the top and bottom rails at the correct distance apart (*no glue in the grooves*). Glue the mortises and tenons and clamp the door using battens between the clamps and the stiles. Check the diagonals for squareness and make sure the door is not in winding. Place a straight edge on the face of the rails across the door to make sure that the stiles are in line with the rails.

Once the glue is set, clean up the front and back of the door, then fit it to the carcase; start by planing the bottom edge true and square then the hinging stile so that it and the bottom conform exactly to the carcase. Then shoot in the top rail and outside stile. Once the edges are cleaned up there should be about a total of 1.5mm ($\frac{1}{16}$″) clearance in length and width for the door. Finally, mark out and cut the recesses for the hinges. If using good-quality solid brass butt hinges, set your router to the thinnest part of one leaf of the hinge, rout out the recess then create the taper by paring with a chisel from the outside of the recess. Once the hinges are screwed to the door, offer it up to the carcase, resting the bottom on a piece of garnet paper to give some clearance, then mark the exact position of the hinges on the carcase with a knife. Cut the recesses in the carcase as in the door and hang the door making sure that it lies in the same plane as the front of the carcase. Cleaning up, fitting and hanging a glazed door is exactly the same as for the solid panel door. Put the glass in last, using beading mitred at the corners. Fix the beading with panel pins, pre-drilling the holes using a headless panel pin as a drill bit in order to avoid splitting. If you fit silvered glass, be very careful not to scratch the back when nailing in the beading.

I leave the design and fixing of the handle to your imagination. Once the handle is on, fix a catch to the door. I use double-ball brass catches since they are more attractive than most magnetic catches.

The choice of polish is up to you. Poly-urethane thinned 50/50 with white spirit applied with a rag in 3 or 4 coats, rubbing down between coats, gives a pleasant, tough finish. Otherwise, you may prefer oil, wax or french polish.

The more experienced cabinetmakers will realize that this design could be modified to give a more demanding project. For instance, the cabinet could be bow-fronted and the judicious use of contrasting lines of inlay on the door frame and/or the carcase could give the design a more superior appearance.

Fig. 10 Gluing-up door. Be sure to measure the diagonals and to check for winding

Cutting List

Overall size: 508 mm(20″) × 381 mm(15″) × 203 mm(8″) deep

Item	No.	Length	Width	Thickness
Sides	2	502 mm $19\frac{3}{4}''$	203 mm 8″	16 mm $\frac{5}{8}''$
Top*	1	384 mm $15\frac{1}{8}''$	203 mm 8″	16 mm $\frac{5}{8}''$
Bottom*	1	384 mm $15\frac{1}{8}''$	203 mm 8″	16 mm $\frac{5}{8}''$
Shelf	1	359 mm $14\frac{1}{8}''$	159 mm $6\frac{1}{4}''$	16 mm $\frac{5}{8}''$
Back	1	486 mm $19\frac{1}{8}''$	359 mm $14\frac{1}{8}''$	6 mm $\frac{1}{4}''$

Plywood, preferably birch.

*1.5 mm($\frac{1}{16}''$) extra allowed on each end of top and bottom for overhang of endgrain which is cleaned up after carcase is glued-up.

Door: Overall size: 476 mm(18$\frac{3}{4}''$) × 350 mm(13$\frac{3}{4}''$) × 22 mm($\frac{7}{8}''$)

Item	No.	Length	Width	Thickness
Stiles*	2	480 mm $18\frac{7}{8}''$	46 mm $1\frac{3}{4}''$	22 mm $\frac{7}{8}''$
Rails	2	312 mm $12\frac{1}{4}''$	57 mm $2\frac{1}{4}''$	22 mm $\frac{7}{8}''$
Door panel	1	375 mm $14\frac{3}{4}''$	274 mm $10\frac{3}{4}''$	16 mm $\frac{5}{8}''$
or				
Piece glass	1	cut to fit into rebate with 3 mm ($\frac{1}{8}''$) clearance on width and length.		

*1.5 mm ($\frac{1}{16}''$) extra allowed on each end of stiles for overhang of endgrain which is cleaned up after door is glued-up.

13. Bracket Clock

Harold Babb

SINCE first making this little clock ten years ago, various minor design changes have been incorporated and much of the work can now be done with the router.

The choice of material for this project is a very personal matter; having made this clock in numerous hard and soft woods I favour mahogany as it seems to enhance the simple but attractive lines of the design. However, this decision must be left to the maker.

The overall sizes are 317 × 254 × 155mm (12½″ × 10″ × 6⅛″) and it is designed to accommodate the R5S Hermle Westminster Chime 8 day movement with the 13100 11 200 × 200 dial, available from Charles Greville & Co., Willey

Mill House, Alton Road, Farnham, Surrey, GU1 5EL who also supply brass handles, hinges and catches. No doubt other movements can be used but the maker should ensure the sizes are compatible with the chosen movement before commencing the project.

The base and top are the same, measuring 240 × 146 × 16mm (9 $\frac{7}{16}$″ × 5¾″ × ⅝″), with 10 × 6mm (⅜″ × ¼″) grooves for sides and dial board and an 11 × 6mm ($\frac{7}{16}$″ × ¼″) rebate for the back door, as shown in Fig. 2. Form a 6mm (¼″) ovolo moulding on the top edge of the base board around the front and two sides (see Fig. 3).

The side sections are 243 × 127 × 16mm

121

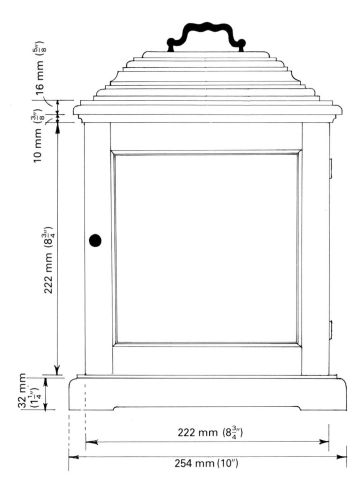

16 mm $\left(\frac{5}{8}''\right)$

10 mm $\left(\frac{3}{8}''\right)$

222 mm $\left(8\frac{3}{4}''\right)$

32 mm $\left(1\frac{1}{4}''\right)$

222 mm $\left(8\frac{3}{4}''\right)$

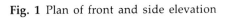

254 mm (10")

Fig. 1 Plan of front and side elevation

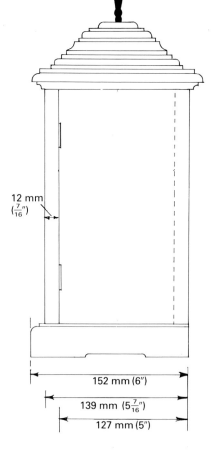

12 mm $\left(\frac{7}{16}''\right)$

152 mm (6")

139 mm $\left(5\frac{7}{16}''\right)$

127 mm (5")

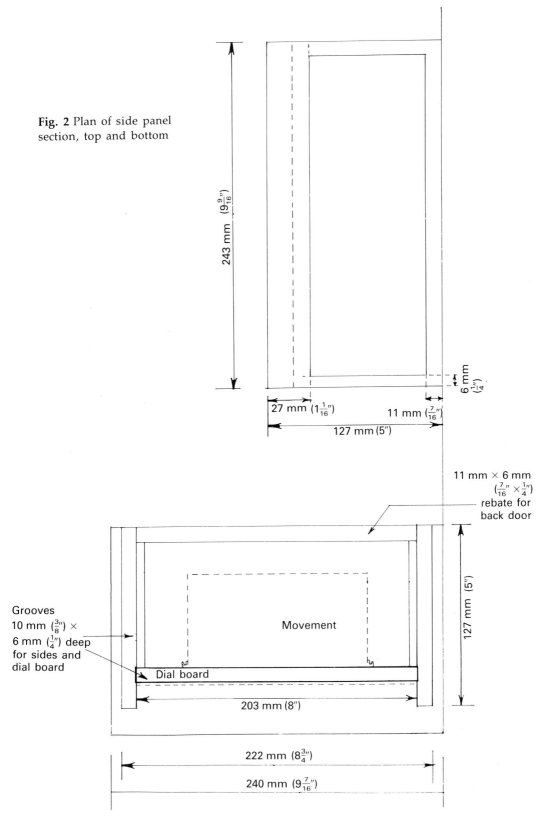

Fig. 2 Plan of side panel section, top and bottom

243 mm $(9\frac{9}{16}")$

6 mm $(\frac{1}{4}")$

27 mm $(1\frac{1}{16}")$

11 mm $(\frac{7}{16}")$

127 mm (5")

11 mm × 6 mm $(\frac{7}{16}" \times \frac{1}{4}")$ rebate for back door

127 mm (5")

Grooves 10 mm $(\frac{3}{8}")$ × 6 mm $(\frac{1}{4}")$ deep for sides and dial board

Movement

Dial board

203 mm (8")

222 mm $(8\frac{3}{4}")$

240 mm $(9\frac{7}{16}")$

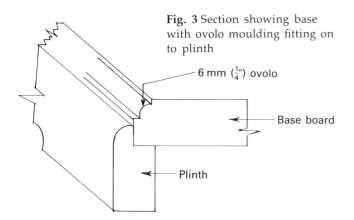

Fig. 3 Section showing base with ovolo moulding fitting on to plinth

6 mm ($\frac{1}{4}''$) ovolo

Base board

Plinth

($9\frac{9}{16}'' \times 5'' \times \frac{5}{8}''$), with a 6×6mm ($\frac{1}{4}'' \times \frac{1}{4}''$) rebate at top and bottom and an 11×6mm ($\frac{7}{16}'' \times \frac{1}{4}''$) rebate one side and a 27×6mm ($1\frac{1}{16}'' \times \frac{1}{4}''$) one on the other edge; this wide recess fits behind and supports the dial board. The dial board is $243 \times 203 \times 10$mm ($9\frac{9}{16}'' \times 8'' \times \frac{3}{8}''$) which can be ply or solid wood to match the exterior, both the dial and movement are attached to it, so it needs to be good, sound material.

The moulded top is made up of four sections of solid wood. The largest one is $210 \times 114 \times 16$mm ($8\frac{1}{4}'' \times 4\frac{1}{2}'' \times \frac{5}{8}''$) with all edges on one face being moulded with a 10mm ($\frac{3}{8}''$) ovolo router bit. The second section is $179 \times 84 \times 16$mm ($7\frac{1}{16}'' \times 3\frac{5}{16}'' \times \frac{5}{8}''$) and moulded with a 10mm ($\frac{3}{8}''$) round bit to form an opposite shape to the previous one. The third piece is $152 \times$

56×16mm ($6'' \times 2\frac{3}{16}'' \times \frac{5}{8}''$) and moulded with a 10mm ($\frac{3}{8}''$) ovolo bit. The fourth and smallest part is $121 \times 25 \times 10$mm ($4\frac{3}{4}'' \times 1'' \times \frac{3}{8}''$) and for this a 6mm ($\frac{1}{4}''$) round over bit is used, thus making an attractive top to the case.

The only problem with this method of construction is the fixing of the brass handle to the top. This can be overcome by counter boring through the two lower sections after gluing all four pieces together. Use a 25mm (1") bit then bore the remainder with a drill bit to suit screw sizes in the handle.

The alternative to this, which I prefer as no end grain is exposed, is to machine one piece $711 \times 29 \times 16$mm ($28'' \times 1\frac{1}{8}'' \times \frac{5}{8}''$) and one piece $457 \times 29 \times 16$mm ($18'' \times 1\frac{1}{8}'' \times \frac{5}{8}''$) both with a 10mm ($\frac{3}{8}''$) ovolo on one edge, and one piece $609 \times 29 \times 16$mm ($24'' \times 1\frac{1}{8}'' \times \frac{5}{8}''$) on one edge with a 10mm ($\frac{3}{8}''$) round bit. The fourth section is the same as for the solid top. Mitre these together to form sections to sizes as given for solid pieces. This also overcomes the problem of fixing the handle to the top. (See Fig. 6)

Having decided which method to use, carry out the necessary work and assemble. Clean up and fit the handle, then place on top of the case in the centre, mark lightly round it and mask this centre area on the clock top. Remove handle before applying finish of your choice, but do not yet fix the top to the case.

Fig. 4 Rear view of base, one side and back board

Fig. 5 Sections for solid top being moulded by the router

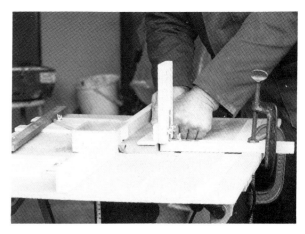

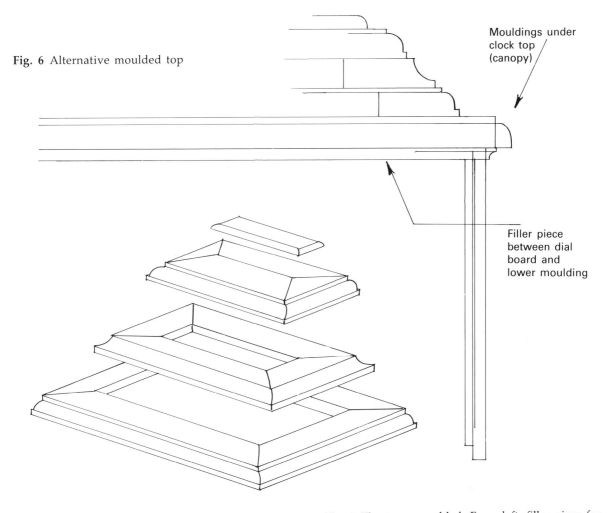

Fig. 6 Alternative moulded top

Mouldings under clock top (canopy)

Filler piece between dial board and lower moulding

Fig. 7 Solid moulded sections which form the top (shown with part-assembled base, side and back board)

Fig. 8 The top assembled. From left, filler piece for top front, two pieces of plinth, two pieces of moulding for underside of top and two pieces of moulding for edge of top board

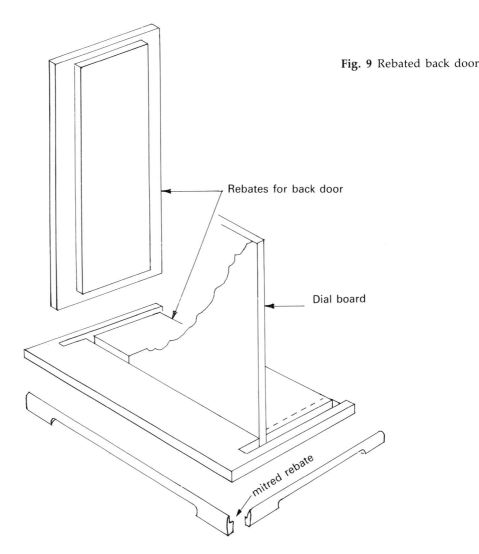

Fig. 9 Rebated back door

Rebates for back door

Dial board

mitred rebate

Make the back door from 22 × 11mm ($\frac{7}{8}''$ × $\frac{7}{16}''$) section material with a 3mm ($\frac{1}{8}''$) groove, 6mm ($\frac{1}{4}''$) deep along the centre of one edge. The top and bottom rails have 6mm × 3mm ($\frac{1}{4}''$ × $\frac{1}{8}''$) tongues to fit into grooves in stiles with a 3mm ($\frac{1}{8}''$) ply panel fitted into the grooves and veneered to match the solid wood used for the rest of the case. This will hold the door square and rigid. The size of the door is 241 × 203mm ($9\frac{1}{2}''$ × 8'') overall, hung on two 25mm (1'') brass butts, and having a 6mm ($\frac{1}{4}''$) ball catch in the shutting edge and a striking plate in the side of the case. Fit a small drop-ring handle for opening.

The front door is made from 30 × 11mm ($1\frac{3}{16}''$ × $\frac{7}{16}''$) solid wood, butt jointed & dowelled

with one 6mm ($\frac{1}{4}''$) dowel at each corner, taking care to keep the dowel clear of the rebate and moulding.

After assembly and when the glue has cured, the moulding is formed with a 3mm ($\frac{1}{8}''$) ovolo cutter and a rebate 6 × 6mm ($\frac{1}{4}''$ × $\frac{1}{4}''$) on the inner surface with a straight cutter. The overall size of the door is 222 × 222mm ($8\frac{3}{4}''$ × $8\frac{3}{4}''$), hung on two 25mm (1'') brass butts and secured with a small brass side hook.

If preferred, another method for making this door is by forming both rebate and moulding on one continuous length of 30 × 11mm ($1\frac{3}{16}''$ × $\frac{7}{16}''$) timber 914mm (36'') long; form the joints by mitring the mouldings on the top and bottom rails and cutting away the mouldings

126

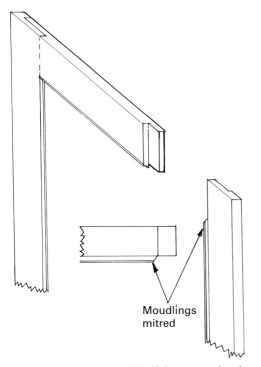

Moudlings mitred

Fig. 10 Diagram – stopped half lap joint for front door

on the stiles to a mitre to receive the rails; use a stopped half lap joint glued and screwed on the inner surface.

With doors of this thickness it is difficult to form a rebate deep enough to take the glass and a glazing bead, so the accepted method in this case is to put the glass in dry and fix with sprigs. Do not use a hammer when doing this as it is very easy to break the glass, use a firmer chisel with the bevel on the glass; this is much safer, and it is kinder to the fingers.

There are two separate mouldings at the edge of the top section, one 13×10mm ($\frac{1}{2}'' \times \frac{3}{8}''$) rounded over once, attached flush at the bottom on the front and two sides. The other is smaller, being 10×8mm ($\frac{3}{8}'' \times \frac{5}{16}''$) which is formed by using a 6mm ($\frac{1}{4}''$) round bit, and is fixed at the junction of the side members and top. At the front it will be necesary to fix a filler piece under the top $222 \times 29 \times 10$mm ($8\frac{3}{4}'' \times 1\frac{1}{8}'' \times \frac{3}{8}''$), notched round the side sections to provide a fixing for the front section of the moulding.

The plinth is of 32×16mm ($1\frac{1}{4}'' \times \frac{5}{8}''$) section, preferably machined in a 610mm (2') length with an 8mm ($\frac{5}{16}''$) lebate 8mm ($\frac{5}{16}''$) deep on the inner top edge, using a 8mm ($\frac{5}{16}''$) straight cutter. The outer top edge is formed with a 10mm ($\frac{3}{8}''$) round over bit. The cutaway on the under side is formed with a 10mm ($\frac{3}{8}''$) straight bit. This will need to be carefully set out prior to cutting mitres, to ensure that the feet on all corners are the same length, ideally 38mm ($1\frac{1}{2}''$).

Having prepared all the sections and assembled the case, before fitting the doors and moulded top, you will find it better to fit the dial and movement. The simplest way to do this, after checking that the holes in the dial fit the movement, is to place the dial in the aperture, mark holes on the dial board, and drill the holes. To fix the dial, I prefer to drill all four corners and countersink four 10mm ($\frac{3}{8}''$) No. 2 screws, rather than stick the dial to the board. When fixed, turn the clock face down, locate the movement over holes and fix in place. Fit a block 29mm ($1\frac{1}{8}''$) thick to receive the gong, as directed by the instructions sent with the movement. Remove the dial and movement, fit and fix doors and then apply the finish of your choice. Re-fix the handle to the top and, after removing masking from case, glue the top in position. Replace dial and movement.

14. Tea Tray

Dean Harvey and Adela Sadler

THIS design highlights the use of the router as an aid to turning and demonstrates again the versatility of this machine. We recommend that this solid wood tea tray be made in ash, a versatile and easy to work material which machines well and is ideal for this type of project.

To make the tray you will need all the wood on the cutting list at finished sizes, together with the turning jig which can be made from solid wood or a man-made board. The imperial equivalent measurements in brackets are approximate, so work in either metric or imperial throughout the project; do not mix

the two systems when measuring and marking out. The router-cutters you will need are a 6mm ($\frac{1}{4}''$) straight cutter and a 3mm ($\frac{1}{8}''$) radius round over cutter.

Step 1:   To make the tray base. (Fig. 2)
Lay the four pieces of tray bottom out on the work bench and arrange for the best possible grain and colour match; mark a pencil line across the arranged wood to indicate the face side.

To make the groove for the loose tongue joint, set your router for grooving the edges of the boards. To set the correct depth slowly drop

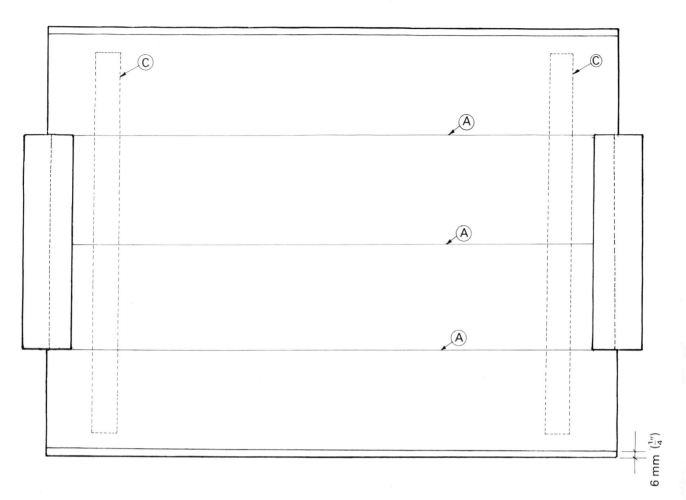

Fig. 1 Third angle projection drawing for the tea tray

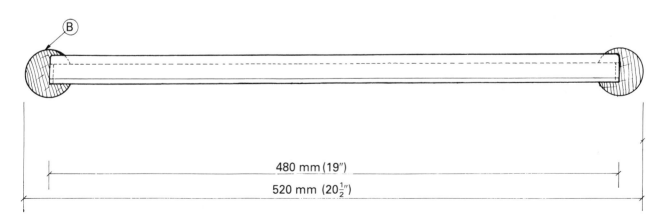

6 mm ($\frac{1}{4}$")

480 mm (19")

520 mm (20$\frac{1}{2}$")

129

Fig. 2

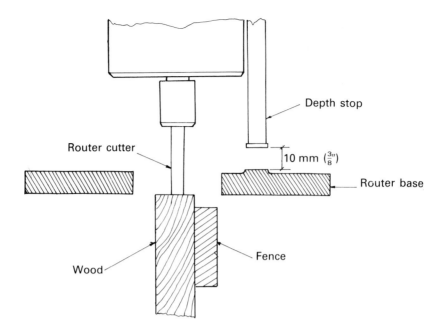

Depth stop

Router cutter

10 mm ($\frac{3}{8}$")

Router base

Wood

Fence

the 6mm ($\frac{1}{4}$") straight cutter onto the wood and adjust the depth stop bar at 10mm ($\frac{3}{8}$") from its stop. Then set the cutter in the centre of the board edge and with the face side against the fence, cut the groove in two 5mm ($\frac{3}{16}$") strokes taking care not to "drop" the router over the edge.

Rout the grooves on each piece keeping the face side to the fence and remembering not to groove the two outer boards on their outer edge. Clean the grooves of any sawdust and then apply the glue to the grooves and fit the three loose tongues. Clamp with two sash clamps across its width and wipe away any excess glue with a damp cloth. Leave to set.

Step 2: Using the turning jig (Fig. 3).
Mark the centre of the wood for the handles by drawing diagonals between its corners and marking the centre. Scribe a 40mm ($1\frac{1}{2}$") diameter circle on the ends and plane off the corners to make the routing a little easier. Mount this wood between the centres of the jig and tighten until the wood feels firmly in place. Attach the router base to the sliding carriage with bolts and slide onto the jig. Horizontal adjustments can be made by making the bolt holes into slots for the router to run in. Drop the router

onto a flat face of the handle and lock into position. Slide the carriage back off the work and switch on the router. Move the router back to the start of the wood and whilst holding the carriage with one hand slowly rotate the work by its handle with the other hand.

Depending on the speed and power of your router, cut a little at a time, making sure that a full rotation is cut each time. Work your way along until you have a round sectioned piece

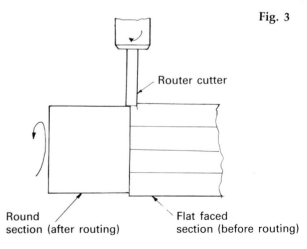

Fig. 3

Router cutter

Round
section (after routing)

Flat faced
section (before routing)

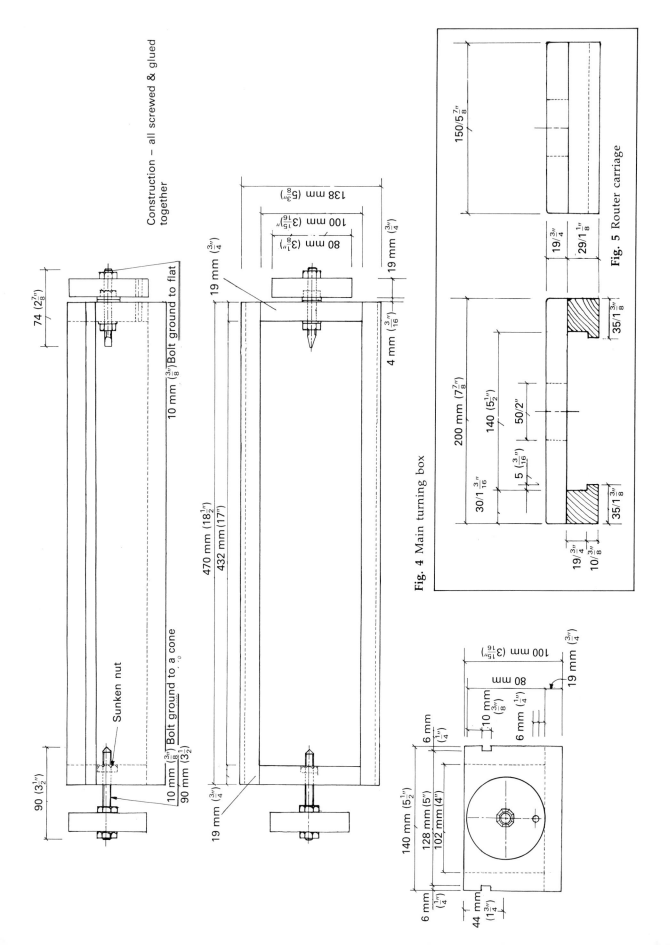

Construction – all screwed & glued together

Fig. 4 Main turning box

Fig. 5 Router carriage

of wood. Be careful to move your router slowly and to rotate the wood into the cutter.

Finish this turning when the diameter of the turned section is exactly 40mm ($1\frac{1}{2}$″).

Step 3:   To groove the handles (Fig. 6).
Drop the cutter onto the work as before and set to rout a 14mm ($\frac{9}{16}$″) deep groove. Lock the work in position with the locking bolt and cut the first groove down the section by simply sliding the carriage along the jig.

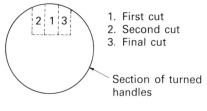

1. First cut
2. Second cut
3. Final cut

Section of turned handles

Fig. 6

Remove the carriage and accurately relocate the router to slide along 6mm ($\frac{1}{4}$″) to the left of the first groove. Mount the carriage back onto the jig and rout the second groove. Repeat this process for the third groove.

You should now have a length of turned wood with an 18mm ($\frac{3}{4}$″) groove. This can now be sanded with 180 grit garnet paper to remove scratches that may have occurred during routing. Convert this length into two handles by cutting in half. Trim each piece to length, 177mm (7″), to remove the wastage and damaged wood. The ends can be cleaned either by hand or with a disc sander.

You should now have two grooved sections of wood, 40mm ($1\frac{1}{2}$″) in diameter and 177mm (7″) in length.

Step 4:   To fit the stiffening battens. (Fig. 7).
The tray base should now be ready to take out of clamps if the glue has set.

Plane the base level on both sides, taking care not to take away too much. After levelling, clamp the tray base to the work bench, reverse side up, and set your router to groove a housing for the stiffening battens. Use the router fence for this operation, making several cuts, to end up with a groove 314mm ($12\frac{1}{2}$″) long, 20mm ($\frac{3}{4}$″) wide and 6mm ($\frac{1}{4}$″) deep, stopped 10mm ($\frac{3}{8}$″) from each side. Carry out this operation on both ends of the board.

You will be routing across the grain this time, however, so take your time to make the cut, whilst making sure the cutter does not burn. The uneven end to the groove should be squared up with a chisel.

The battens can now be fitted into the housing, by fitting one end and then scribing

Fig. 7

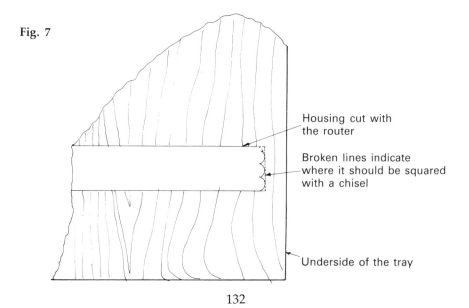

Housing cut with the router

Broken lines indicate where it should be squared with a chisel

Underside of the tray

the battens to length. Cut to length and glue into place. Clamp the whole item onto a flat surface and wipe away the excess glue with the damp cloth. When the glue has set, the battens can be planed flush with the surface, and the whole piece sanded smooth.

Step 5:   To fit the tray lippings. (Figs. 8, 9 & 10).

We are now ready to rebate the sides of the tray to accept the lippings. Set your router to cut a 6mm ($\frac{1}{4}$") rebate and work with your cutter cutting clockwise into the wood. A rebate like this will normally need two to three cuts to achieve the required 12mm ($\frac{1}{2}$") depth.

With the rebate now cut, we are ready to round over the lipping on the top edge, and this must be done with the 3mm ($\frac{1}{8}$") radius round over cutter. For this operation we need a router table to allow us to use the router as a spindle moulder.

Line up the table fence with the pilot on the cutter as shown. Get the cutter level with the surface of the router table. Test the setting on

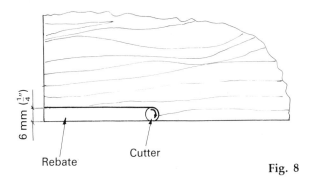

6 mm ($\frac{1}{4}$")

Rebate   Cutter

Fig. 8

a scrap piece of wood and when the cutter is set correctly the fences can be positioned.

With the second fence set at the width of one of the lippings use a couple of push sticks to guide the lippings through. Mould both corners of the lippings with the router cutter until an end section is formed as shown. The lippings are sanded smooth and then glued and clamped into the rebates. When the glue has set, trim the ends flush with the ends of the tray, and sand.

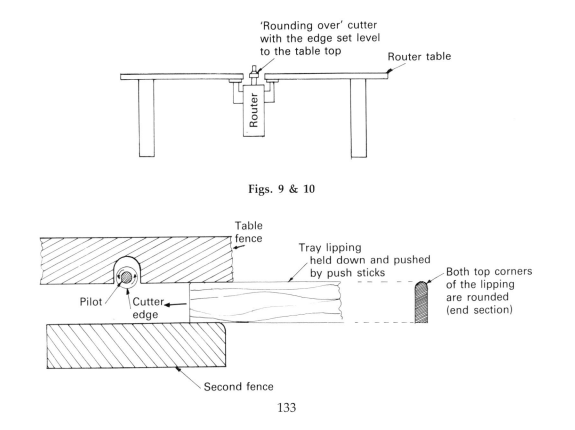

'Rounding over' cutter with the edge set level to the table top

Router table

Router

Figs. 9 & 10

Table fence

Tray lipping held down and pushed by push sticks

Both top corners of the lipping are rounded (end section)

Pilot   Cutter edge

Second fence

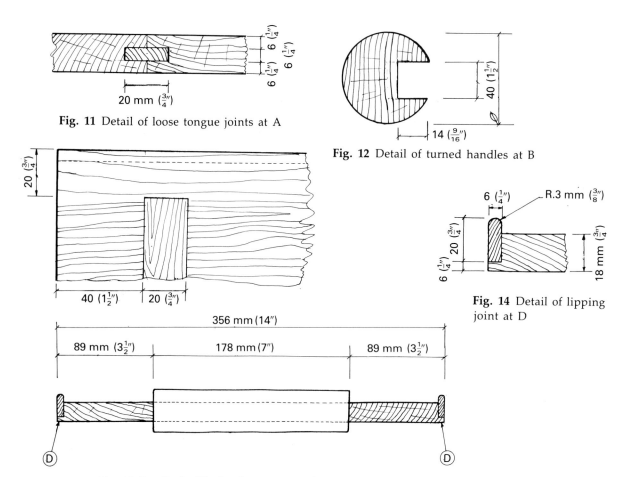

Fig. 11 Detail of loose tongue joints at A

20 mm (¾″)

6 (¼″)
6 (¼″)
6 (¼″)
6 (¼″)

Fig. 12 Detail of turned handles at B

40 (1½″)

14 (9/16″)

20 (¾″)

40 (1½″)   20 (¾″)

6 (¼″)   R.3 mm (⅜″)

20 (¾″)
6 (¼″)

18 mm (¾″)

Fig. 14 Detail of lipping joint at D

356 mm (14″)

89 mm (3½″)   178 mm (7″)   89 mm (3½″)

Ⓓ   Ⓓ

Fig. 13 Detail of stiffening batten on underside at C

Step 6:   To fit the handles. (Fig. 15).
Rout a small housing the length of the handles, on the ends of the tray. Fit the handles onto the ends and position centrally. Scribe a line on the end grain of the tray base at each side and pencil a line on the top surface so you can see how long to make the cut.

Set the router with its 6mm (¼″) straight cutter to cut a 6mm (¼″) wide rebate, but this time cut the full depth of the tray, keeping within the pencil lines. Square the corners of the rebate with a chisel and fit the handle into position.

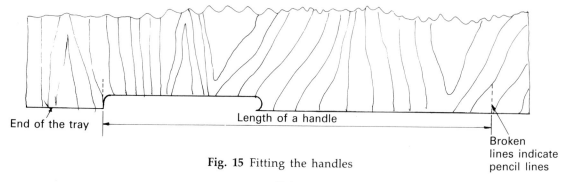

End of the tray

Length of a handle

Broken lines indicate pencil lines

Fig. 15 Fitting the handles

134

If it fits comfortably, secure with glue and clamp. When set, finally sand with 220 grit paper.

Step 7:   To finish the tray.
To finish, we recommend a pre-catalysed mela- mine lacquer. Apply the first coat, ideally with a spray gun or with a rag. When dry "de-nib" with 280 grit paper. Coat again and when dry de-nib with 0000 wire wool. Repeat this final process and de-nib with the wire wool.

Cutting List

Item	No.	Length	Width	Thickness
Tray bottoms	4	480mm 19″	89mm $3\frac{1}{2}''$	18mm $\frac{3}{4}''$
Tray handles	1	380mm 15″	40mm $1\frac{1}{2}''$	40mm $1\frac{1}{2}''$
Lippings	2	480mm 19″	20 mm $\frac{3}{4}''$	6mm $\frac{1}{4}''$
Stiffening battens	2	316mm $12\frac{1}{2}''$	20mm $\frac{3}{4}''$	6mm $\frac{1}{4}''$
Loose tongues	3	480mm 19″	20mm $\frac{3}{4}''$	6mm $\frac{1}{4}''$

All measurements in metric, millimetres followed by approximate imperial inches.

A Chinese General pulling an arrow out of the
forequarters of the horse belonging to Emperor T'ai
tsung circa 630 A.D.

The original stone panel is in the
University Museum, Philadelphia

15. Carving with a Miniature Router

Eric Collins

THE choice of a subject suitable for carving
with a miniature router needs careful study in
order to keep within the range of its capabilities,
including the ease with which it can be
controlled. The main restrictions are the shape
and size of the cutters, the precision with which
you can adjust the depth of cut and the degree
of visibility around the cutter. The maximum
depth of the subject which you are going to
carve must not exceed the maximum depth of
cut afforded by your router and there must be
sufficient space for your cutters to work between
different figures and objects etc.

The choice of subject for this project is a low
relief copy of a stone panel taken from the
tomb of a 7th century Chinese emperor showing
a T'ang horse and warrior. The wood selected
was a piece of cherry.

The panel was planed flat and true and then
sanded and wire wool polished. A standard
router was used with a 3mm ($\frac{1}{8}''$) single fluted
cutter to make a trench round the outline of
the horse and the border to act as a guide for
the future removal of the waste wood and to
prevent any accidental removal of the edges of
the carving when the time came to remove the
waste.

The technique I adopted for most of the

remainder of the carving is, as far as I am aware, applicable only to the de luxe Dremel router attachment which only fits the Dremel range of drills. It is ideally suitable for relief carving as it can be controlled with ease using one hand only and, because it can be so accurately and easily adjusted to give an infinitely variable depth of cut, it is possible to use it as one would a paintbrush.

Where, for example, I wanted to carve a slow convex slope, I estimated the final depth of cut needed, set this on the gauge, then, resting the router on its back edge with the cutter just touching the wood where I wanted the curve to start, I moved the router slowly towards the finishing point gradually applying increasing pressure until the desired shape had been obtained.

Concave hollows were made using the same technique but in the reverse order. It tends to be a slow process and those unfamiliar with this router should take the precaution of practising on scrap pieces of the same wood as the carving to accurately get the feel of the process.

You need to know before starting how hard the wood is, the way in which the grain reacts to the cutters and the amount of pressure you need to reproduce the shapes you want. This parallels the Chinese attitude of spending hours grinding their inks to get them the right colour and to concentrate their mind on the activity they were going to undertake.

Carving along edges requires confidence but since the Dremel is so easily controlled and accurate it is quite easy to cut up to a line and to move along it without moving across it. For want of a better word, "contour" cutting can be used to cut convex slopes. This can be done by using the miniature cutters in the Minicraft range. These require about 10mm ($\frac{3}{8}$") to be ground off their shafts to reduce their length to that of the Dremel bits. (A range of collets suitable for these bits is available.) The technique used is to mark the inner edge of the slope with pencil first of all and then outline it lightly with a 1mm veiner to provide a slight edge to work against. (Too deep a cut will leave an unsightly groove which is difficult to remove.) Then a very light cut is made with a vertical edged cutter along the desired length of the line and successive cuts, getting progressively deeper and further apart, are made until the outside edge and required depth are reached.

Having chosen the subject, I had to decide on the scale to use. Had this been a freehand carving, this would not have been so important but what I had to take into consideration was the fact that the original panel is lifesize and the perspective used to carve it is different from that now used in the west, so, any desire to alter it to conventional perspective had to be resisted. It is also necessary to remember that since the original carvings were in a tomb and when shown to the Emperor would have been visible only by the dim light of oil lamps, the carvers would have taken this factor into consideration when they decided on the depth of cut they were going to use on the panels, for light played an important part in the perspective used by Chinese carvers.

I estimated from the warrior's height, say 1753mm (5'9"), a 1/10th scale, making the finished panel size 305 × 255mm (12" × 10") and the warrior's height 178mm (7"). Since the maximum depth of cut of the Dremel is 8mm ($\frac{5}{16}$") I restricted the depth of cut to 6mm ($\frac{1}{4}$"). The panel was 22mm ($\frac{7}{8}$") thick.

I cut out two photocopies of the panel. One was mounted on a piece of wood quite loosely so that the edges showed up in relief, and the other, on a piece of plywood from which I made a fairly accurate template. I say "fairly accurate" quite deliberately as I wanted to study the somewhat indistinct reproduction carefully as I filed and sandpapered it to its final shape. This was important as the photograph contained a lot of outline shadow which had to be removed to reveal the correct outlines. Further study of the T'ang horse's distinctive shape was made from pottery and other examples I could find.

Then I made a tracing of the "corrected" panel, which isolated the figures from their background, and transferred the tracing onto the wood with carbon paper.

Before you finally transfer any design to the wood, carefully study the grain and features

Fig. 1 Making a cut-out of the figures to isolate them from the background

Fig. 2 The final tracing with all shadows removed

138

and move the tracing over the panel to give you the best possible advantages for your carving. This is an essential procedure when working in relief, especially when one is artificially restricted to the amount of depth of cut one can use. In my carving the grain structure on the horse's hindquarters and the armoured skirt worn by the warrior show the advantage of planning the work carefully.

Once I had decided where to place the tracing I used an old ball point pen to make the lines show up clearly and cleanly on the wood. The carving was held in a bench holdfast throughout, with a piece of protective ply.

There is a lengthy operation of resolving the routing sequence; in determining the highlights and "danger" areas and other places where there is a risk of error. Use the tracings and template to help with this work.

With a carving project that is assisted by a router you will always have to decide whether to start by routing away the waste areas first, followed by the more detailed carving work, or vice versa. The small router allows a good deal of visibility around the cutter area during the progress of the work but obviously care must be taken when working near to the design outlines. I decided to do as much of the carving as I could, leaving the waste for as long as possible to give me a flat platform to work from.

First I outlined the man with a 1mm veiner and then routed him flat by approximately 1.5mm ($\frac{1}{16}''$). (The Dremel has gradation marks at 1.5mm ($\frac{1}{16}''$) intervals marked on its side and each complete turn of the adjusting wheel affords a 0.75mm ($\frac{1}{32}''$) adjustment, with, of course, any other amount desired.) I thought this reduction in his thickness would compensate for the difference in depth between him and the horse.

It is important to note at this stage that any outline you cut around the outside of a figure must be to its final carving depth. If you do not do this and decide at a later stage to take the outline deeper you are liable to lose your outline and the freshness of your original cut. It also adds to the problems which will confront you when you come to the final stage of

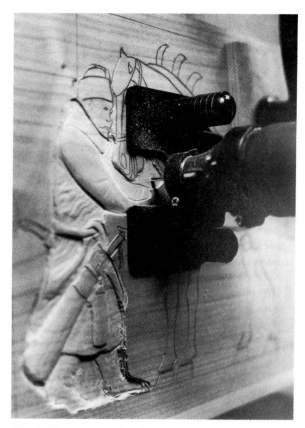

Fig. 3 The router, showing its size and the visibility it affords around the cutter

cleaning the carving, as you are liable to get more wiry fibres around the outline than you do when you make a single clean cut. Any alteration to the depth of cut can affect the perspective you are trying to achieve and once you start to try to overcome any mistakes you have made you usually find you make things look worse than they were.

The softness required for his skin coat and soft felt boots was achieved by using 400 wet and dry and 0000 wire wool. The folds in his coat were made with a burr but his face and hands and the final edging were done with chisels.

The horse was outlined in the same way but its body was left at surface level. Its four legs were, however, proportionally reduced to the flat surfaces with the router to obtain the necessary perspective. A burr was used on them to show the muscles and tendons running down its legs. The reins and other accoutrements were carefully marked out with the veiner and the areas up to them reduced with the router.

I used the "painting" technique to get the saddle cloth to follow the contours of the horse's body and to make it look less wooden than chiselling would have made it. The borders to the saddle cloth and the saddle itself presented no problems to the Dremel. The most difficult part of all was getting the forequarters of the horse right because of the reins and I had to be constantly on the alert not to cut across one of them. This inhibited the free flowing shape of the muscles which I had hoped to achieve but gouges were used to good effect to overcome the problem.

It was possible to rout the horse's neck to shape around the area of the throat and as far as its major neck muscles. Its head and accompanying war bonnet had to be chiselled and this is where the very fine hard traced outlines came into their own.

The eye was shaped with a 2mm ($\frac{1}{16}$") gouge. I made two hard cuts to shape the oval and two light cuts to remove the waste. As I had carved the face before the ears, the positioning of them had to be carefully worked out to keep them square to the head and the direction in which the horse was looking. Horse's ears are not difficult to shape. The easiest way to picture

Fig. 4 Waste removed from between hind legs prior to routing offside rear leg

Fig. 5 Leg routed down to correct depth. Underbelly area not cut so deeply as it is required for muscle. Hooves not cut until last as they are on the same level but not the same depth

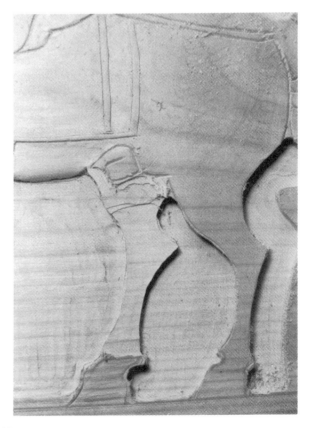

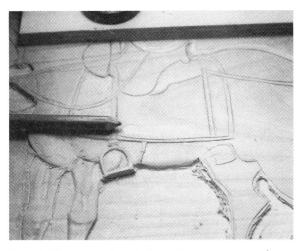

Fig. 6 Close-up of 'paintbrush' cut, moving from right to left. Tip of pencil shows deepest part of cut

them is to envisage a cone with a triangular portion cut out of its front. The mouth was outlined with a 1mm veiner and completed with a 1mm gouge.

All the relief carvings I could find of horses of this period show them with large hooves and with the hind legs in the position shown in the carving, and this trait was still shown in surviving examples of Mongolian paintings of the 13th century. Much of Chinese art was stylised and formalised very early in their history and, whilst this is not the place to discuss Chinese art, it is perhaps pertinent to point out that they did not and do not paint or draw in the traditional method employed in the west. They only use a single stroke with

Fig. 7 Saddle and cloth partly routed. 'Paintbrush' technique being used to give roundness. Slight marks visible running from inner band to right towards stirrup leather

Fig. 8 Preliminary work on the warrior and the horse's head

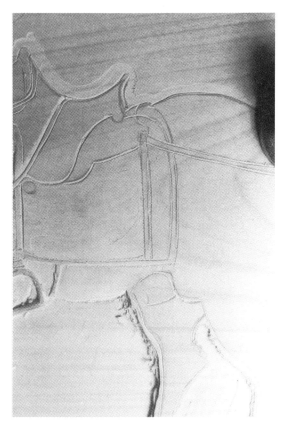

the speed of a "startled snake" for both outline and detail and it is interesting to speculate if the artist who drew the outlines on this series of panels used the same technique and if this contributed to the shape of the horse.

I overcame the problem of needing a flat base to operate from, when I was routing over an area which had already been carved, by making two separate platforms which extended over the width of the carving. I used a 5mm ($\frac{3}{16}''$) ply for the Dremel and 9mm ($\frac{3}{8}''$) ply for the large router. This gave me sufficient space around the cutters to see where I wanted to make the necessary cuts.

Lighting plays a most important part in relief carving for one has to consider not only the source of light necessary to carve by, but just as important, where the finished carving is going to hang. These two factors have to be taken into consideration from the outset because it is no use carving with a single light source from the top if your carving is going to be illuminated by side lighting. The reason why this factor has to be taken into consideration is that as you carve, shall we say using top lighting, all your carving is unconsciously geared to producing the most striking effect using that light source. If you use several different light sources, then the shadows become diffused and it becomes virtually impossible to produce a dynamic effect, or even to see where you are carving, with any degree of accuracy.

I used a single Anglepoise lamp for the entire project as it gave me shadow exactly where I wanted it. I also found that a stiff brush was necessary to brush the accumulations of sawdust out of the cracks so that I could clearly see where the shadows were falling and if the cuts needed deepening.

Complete the carving by cleaning it free of the marks on the waste produced by the routers

Fig. 10 The router being used to cut out background. Router sitting on 9mm ($\frac{3}{8}''$) bridge (platform) to give level surface to work from

Fig. 9 Dremel router used to cut area in between horse's head and neck and between harness. 3mm ($\frac{1}{8}''$) bit used. Router sitting on 'bridge' made from ply. Visibility afforded by Dremel shows up well in this photograph

and the chisels. Use a selection of replaceable blades and a penknife to cut the edges clean. Where possible use very small cutters in the Dremel to undercut those edges which are suitable for this technique. This requires extreme care and the use of the platform mentioned earlier. Also use chisels and riflers to clean the edges and highlights. Finally rub down with 400 grade wet and dry and 0000 wire wool, then brush it very hard to ensure that no dust or fragments of wire are left anywhere. Seal with cellulose filler.

In conclusion I think it would be unwise for anybody to attempt to use the 'paintbrush' technique, which I have described, using a conventional type of router. With the Dremel, it is only 50mm (2″) from the heel of the router to the cutter and the cutter needs to be extended by only a small amount to get the desired shapes. This operation can be repeated if a deeper cut is required. The distance from the heel of a conventional router to the cutter would, in my opinion, require the cutter to be extended beyond the depth for safety and control. Lastly, but perhaps *most importantly*, wear polycarbonate goggles when routing. You can replace bits and even the piece of wood you have spent hours working on, but you cannot replace your eyes.

Cutters used – 10mm ($\frac{3}{8}$″) double, 6mm ($\frac{1}{4}$″) double, 5mm ($\frac{3}{16}$″) double, 3mm ($\frac{1}{8}$″) single.

Dremel de luxe model 229 attached to a Dremel Moto Tool 258. Cutters used: 2mm ($\frac{1}{16}$″) single, 4mm ($\frac{1}{8}$″) double, 5mm ($\frac{3}{16}$″) double, 6mm ($\frac{1}{4}$″) double. Minicraft miniature cutters and burrs.

Dremel burrs used – 114, 124, 134.

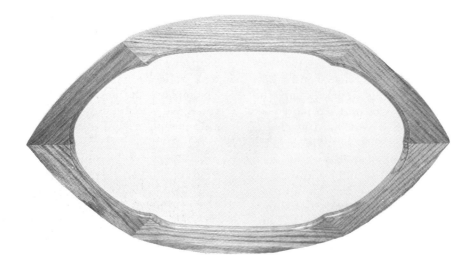

16. Mirror Frame

Fraser Budd

THIS project sets out to provide a simple yet effective solution to an old problem with few constraints and infinite solutions.

The design is an attempt to make the mirror frame subtly more decorative than a standard oval or rectangle, making a feature of the structure and pattern of the grain and the tongue joints. The overall form employs a normally harsh geometric shape which has been softened by incorporating more natural curves.

The example shown was produced in English oak although other hardwoods with good working qualities could be substituted pro-

vided they have a good distinctive grain pattern. The reader could further develop the design during manufacture by cross grain veneering the timber sections prior to the trimming and slotting operations described later.

To commence making the frame first prepare a piece of timber 1700mm (67″) long with square straight edges 80mm (3⅛″) wide and accurately planed to a thickness of 25mm (1″).

From this length of timber the six sections are marked out ready to cut. For economy of timber and to provide the grain matches that are required for this design, see Fig. 1 for the

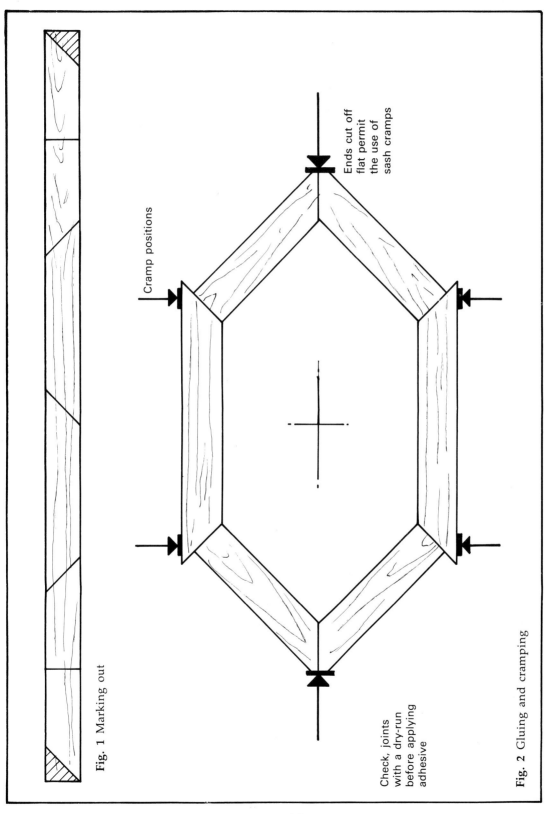

Fig. 1 Marking out

Cramp positions

Ends cut off
flat permit
the use of
sash cramps

Check, joints
with a dry-run
before applying
adhesive

Fig. 2 Gluing and cramping

145

Fig. 3

Fig. 4

suggested layout of the pieces. The marking must be done meticulously using a marking knife, square and mitre square. Errors in accuracy in marking will make planing the ends very difficult. Allow just sufficient waste wood between each piece to enable the saw to pass through and leave 0.5–1mm waste on each end. These can now be planed. This task should only be regarded as complete when each section has been tested for accuracy of angle, (either 45 or 90 degrees), squareness across the end, and when the two side members are exactly the same length; likewise the four angled end pieces. At this point it is essential to realise that only with accurate preparation will the routed joints make up into a gap-free frame and ensure that during the subsequent routing sequence the corners form exactly on the joint lines.

To rout the slots for the tongue joints a 6mm ($\frac{1}{4}''$) thick slotting cutter should be used. However, in order that the slots are not cut to the full depth of the cutter a fence should be used in place of the self following bearing which is part of the usual assembly when using these cutters. If the cutter is too large to allow the manufacturer's fence to be used then one can improvise by clamping a wooden fence onto the table as shown in photo, (Fig. 3). The cutter should be set to the middle of the timber. To ensure that the sections join flush with each other and to cancel out the effect of any inaccuracy in the centring of the cutter make sure that all cuts are routed from the same side.

A face side mark will be of help.

The tongues should be made with the grain running across, not along, (see photo Fig. 4), and must fit snuggly into the slots without gaps as they are visible on the edge of the frame. The parts may now be glued and assembled. (A dry run assembly is recommended. See diagram Fig. 2).

The adhesive used should be brittle setting such as 'Cascomite' as this will help to prevent pulling out the short grain created when the shallow points on the inner profile of the frame at the ends of the joints are formed with the router and when the moulding is run around the edge.

To proceed one should now produce an accurate routing template using 4mm (approx. $\frac{3}{16}''$) ply or hardboard. To achieve the correct shape produce a full-size copy of plan (Fig. 5), drawn on good quality cartridge paper. To cut the profiles a profiling collar should be used attached to the base of the router. When using these collars it is necessary to know accurately the distance between the outer edge of the collar and the edge of the cutter to be used. (Suggested cutter 12mm ($\frac{1}{2}''$)). In order that the cutter will finish to the required size this distance must be subtracted from the outline of the drawing both on the inner and outer profiles. The drawing can now be glued to the plywood, preferably using a fast drying spray-on adhesive, available from drawing office suppliers.

Bandsaw the template to shape and finish

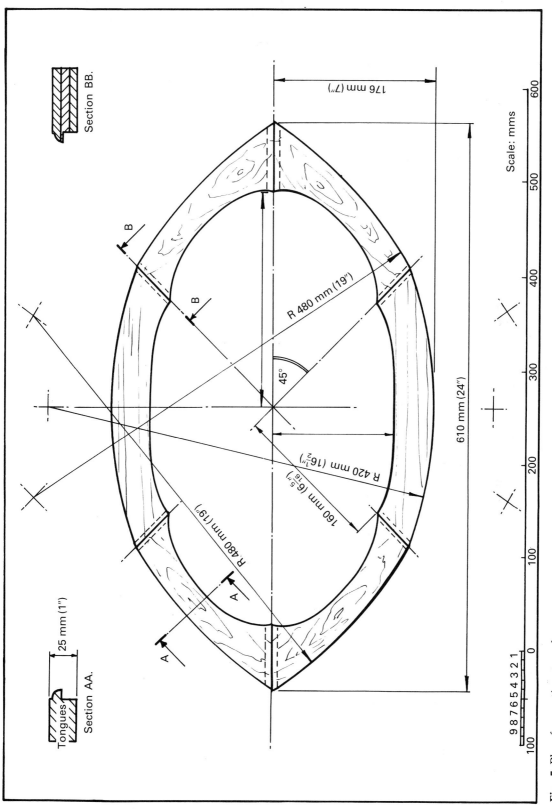

Section BB.

Tongues

25 mm (1")

Section AA.

176 mm (7")

Scale: mms

R 480 mm (19")

45°

610 mm (24")

R 420 mm (16½")

160 mm (6⁵⁄₁₆")

R 480 mm (19")

A

A

B

B

0 100 200 300 400 500 600

9 8 7 6 5 4 3 2 1

0

100

Fig. 5 Plan for routing template

the edges carefully with a spokeshave. To cut the inner profile of the template a jig-saw should be used; if this is not available then the band saw may be used, however, it will be necessary to cut through the template. This cut should be pulled back together, making sure the two sides are in line, and secured with masking tape on both sides.

Having first levelled any unevenness of the joints the template is now placed on the surface of the frame and fixed in place with four or five veneer pins.

The work must now be firmly held down onto the bench whilst the router is run round the template in an anti-clockwise direction cutting away the waste, using three cuts to achieve full depth. The router must be held firmly as it could wobble considerably on the narrow width of the template. If preferred, this operation could be carried out with the router, complete with collar, mounted below the routing table. This would help to keep the router and work more stable. The example shown, however, was completed quite easily using the first suggested method.

To complete the inner shaping the same process is repeated, although to help prevent pulling out bits of the short grain created at the inner ends of the joints as the profile is cut, it is wise to make lighter cuts.

When the general form of the frame has been successfully achieved closely inspect it for irregularities. Before the edge moulding is run round these must all be corrected and a smooth surface created. Produce the moulding using a Trend 7E-2 6mm (¼") cutter with built-in self-follower and carefully rout around the inner face edge. The two things which could easily spoil the job at this late stage are spot burning by the cutter, (the cutter must never be in contact with the work without forward feed); and, as previously mentioned, pulling out the short grain.

The final routing process is to cut a rebate in the back of the frame to receive the mirror and backing panel. On the plan drawing it should be noted that the rebate is not cut right through the tongues but instead a small amount of the thickness of the tongue is left on the lip of the rebate; this amount needs only be about 0.5mm thick. The reason for leaving this is to avoid the router cutter having to remove any of that very delicate short grain. Also, leaving this thin wafer of tongue will strengthen the moulded edge and prevent the possibility of tiny gaps opening.

To cut the rebate, the same slotting cutter as used for the frame slots may be used, but this time the self-follower guide should be used with it. The tool was set up so that the follower bearing could run around the inner moulded edge of the frame. To remove the required thickness of timber after the first cut, the cutter was reassembled to complete a second cut below the first, while the follower still ran against the moulded edge (see photo, Fig. 6). To finish the rebate where the cutter has repeated the points of the inner profile the wood must be pared back to form one smooth continuous curve. The rebate for the mirror should now be elliptical in shape making it an easy job to fit the mirror glass.

Finally the whole frame should be lightly planed over and the holes left by the veneer pins given a drop of water to swell the grain and close them up. The surfaces can be sanded, taking care not to round the corners too much. Three or four coats of sanding sealer lightly rubbed down between coats and finally finished with grade 0000 wire wool and light wax should leave a superb smooth, silky finish.

Fig. 6

17. Lattice Coffee Table

Steve Hallam

THIS project shows how the router can be used to do repetetive operations in a small batch production process, by using simply made jigs.

The table in the photograph is made of ash, though any hardwood can be used. Because the pieces are small in section and in length, a straight grained timber is preferable.

Making the Jigs

The function of the jigs is to hold the item securely whilst it is being routed, and to provide a fence for the router to run against. They are made from any scrap pieces of wood and sheet material (e.g. plywood, chipboard, MDF). There are no measurements on the diagrams of the jigs because only a few sizes are critical.

Jig 1 (Fig. 1)   This jig is used to cut the halving joints and tenons on the lattice pieces. It holds six pieces at one time, which are held in place by two long strips of wood of the same thickness, 16mm ($\frac{5}{8}''$), and by two end stops. It is best to glue and pin the jig together around the pieces to be held, to ensure a good firm fit. The fixed fence has to be placed so that the first crosscut of the router cuts the tenon on

149

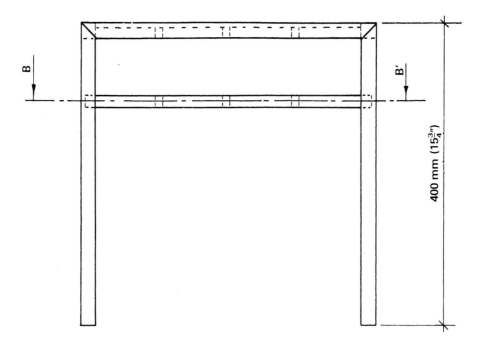

Front and side elevation

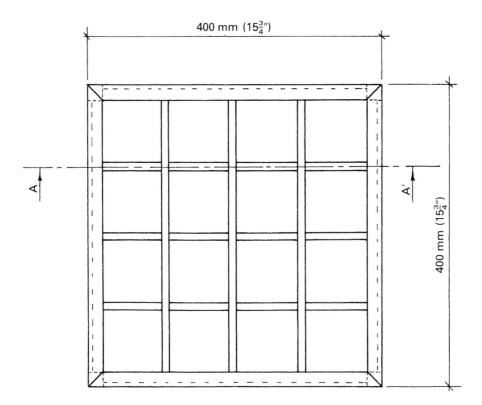

Plan

150

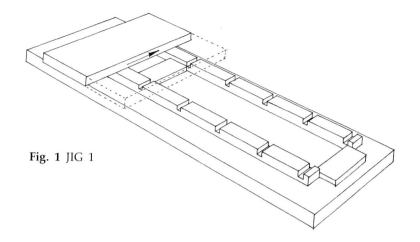

Fig. 1 JIG 1

one end of the lattice pieces. Once the fixed fence is glued on, respective parallel cuts are made by clamping on four spacer blocks to act as new fences for the router to run against. (The first block is shown in dotted lines on the diagram.) The spacer pieces need to be 91.5mm ($3\frac{5}{8}''$) wide and if a long length is accurately planed up, then it can be cut into four pieces of equal width. Make sure that the base board is large enough to be able to clamp it down along the edge of a bench. The jig is made to hold only six pieces, rather than twelve, because on half of the lattice pieces the tenons are on the opposite side to the halvings. This means cutting just the tenons on the second batch of six, and then turning all six over before cutting the halvings.

Jig 2 (Fig. 2) This jig is used to cut the stopped slot mortises in the rails, into which the lattice tenons will fit. It is made to take a single top rail placed upside down, and has a strip of wood pinned to the back edge acting as a stop for the router. This strip is positioned so that the router cuts a slot 14mm ($\frac{9}{16}''$) long, using the 10mm ($\frac{3}{8}''$) straight cutter. This slot is left round-ended, so that when the tenon is in position a half-circle hole will be left open. This is later filled by a strip of wood routed in after the frames are glued up. The fixed fence is placed so that the three mortise slots are cut centrally on the rails (which are 20mm ($\frac{13}{16}''$) oversize in length at this stage) using two of the same spacer blocks used with Jig 1.

The lower rail mortises are also cut in this

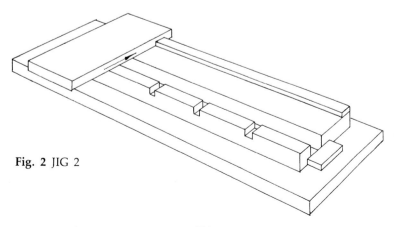

Fig. 2 JIG 2

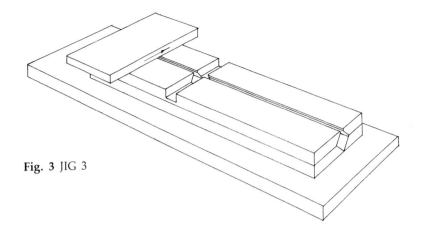

Fig. 3 JIG 3

jig, but two packing strips 6mm ($\frac{1}{4}''$) thick are needed to bring the smaller section lower rails up to the same height and held towards the front of the jig.

Jig 3 (Fig. 3) This jig is used to cut the lower rail joint in the leg by holding the leg on its edge at 45°. It is made from four pieces of 15mm ($\frac{5}{8}''$) plywood, each with a 45° bevel on one edge. It is glued together so that the leg is held in a firm but sliding fit. The end stop under the fence can be glued in place, but the other one will have to be clamped in place, so that the leg can be taken out. The fixed fence is glued on so that the 16mm ($\frac{5}{8}''$) crosscut is in the correct position on the leg.

Jig 4 (Fig. 4) This is a simple 45° jig for cutting the grooves in the lower rail mitres to take the

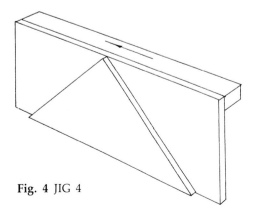

Fig. 4 JIG 4

ply tongues. The router is used with its own fence running off the back edge of the jig. The piece is held by standing the whole jig in the vice. This jig can be used as a 45° shooting board, to plane the mitres on all rails and legs.

Making the Table

1. Using Jig 1 and a 10mm ($\frac{3}{8}''$) straight cutter, cut the lattice halvings and tenons (remembering that half of the lattice pieces have the tenons cut on the opposite side to the halvings). The depth setting of the router is the same for both halvings and tenons, 8mm ($\frac{5}{16}''$).

At this stage the lattices can be sanded and glued up.

2. Using Jig 2 and a 10mm ($\frac{3}{8}''$) cutter, cut the stopped mortise slots in the bottom of the top rails, and then using the packing strips cut the mortise slots in the lower rails.

3. Using Jig 3 and a 16mm ($\frac{5}{8}''$) cutter, cut the lower rail joint in the legs. Then, using a 6mm ($\frac{1}{4}''$) cutter and the same jig, cut a groove 9mm ($\frac{3}{8}''$) deep in the bottom of the 16mm ($\frac{5}{8}''$) groove which will take the ply tongue.

4. Mark out the mitres on all rails and legs, and clean down to the line, using Jig 4 as a shooting board.

5. Using the router with its own fence and a 6mm ($\frac{1}{4}''$) cutter, cut the grooves in the mitres on the rails and legs. The groove is placed 2mm

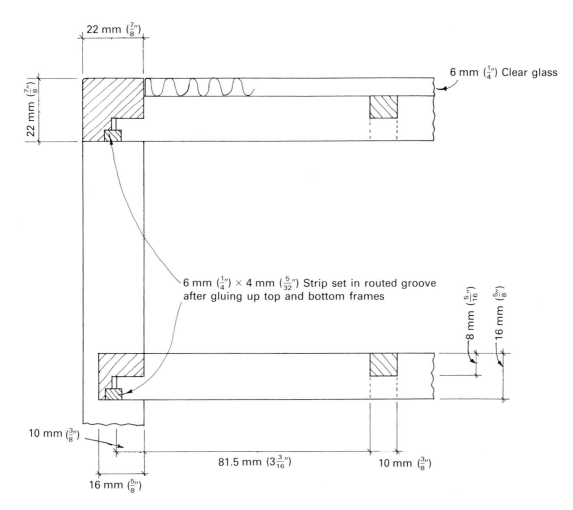

22 mm ($\frac{7}{8}$")

22 mm ($\frac{7}{8}$")

6 mm ($\frac{1}{4}$") Clear glass

6 mm ($\frac{1}{4}$") × 4 mm ($\frac{5}{32}$") Strip set in routed groove after gluing up top and bottom frames

8 mm ($\frac{5}{16}$")

16 mm ($\frac{5}{8}$")

10 mm ($\frac{3}{8}$")

81.5 mm ($3\frac{3}{16}$")

10 mm ($\frac{3}{8}$")

16 mm ($\frac{5}{8}$")

Section on AA': Detail of lattice halvings and lattice/rail tenons: fullsize

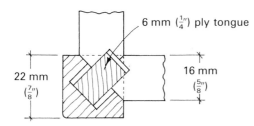

6 mm ($\frac{1}{4}$") ply tongue

22 mm ($\frac{7}{8}$")

16 mm ($\frac{5}{8}$")

Section on BB' showing detail of ply tongue joint between leg and lower rail: fullsize

$\frac{3}{4}$ View of mitred corner joints, showing position of routed groove for ply tongue (not to scale)

Fig. 5

$(\frac{3}{32}'')$ from the edge, and is made as long and deep as possible. Do all the routing with the fence running off the inside faces.

6. Using Jig 4, a 6mm $(\frac{1}{4}'')$ cutter and the router's own fence, cut the grooves in the lower rail mitres to take the tongue which goes into the legs. This groove must be exactly in the middle of the rail, to line up with the groove cut in the leg using Jig 3.

7. After checking that the mitres go up with the tongues in dry, and that the lattices fit into the rails, glue up the top and lower frames. When gluing up the lower frame, do not put any glue in the mitre. This is to allow the corners to be cut off at 45° and dry fitted into the leg joints with a loose tongue. When the tongue is glued in position, at a later stage, the action of cramping the frame to the leg will hold the mitre up.

8. Using the router with its fence and a 6mm $(\frac{1}{4}'')$ cutter, rout a groove 4mm $(\frac{5}{32}'')$ deep in the bottom of the rails on each frame. This groove cuts through the half-circles left at the end of the mortise slots. Glue in the strips and plane down flush; clean down the ends of the strips in the mitres.

9. Dry fit the whole table together and check that everything fits and cramps up tight. Adjust the leg mitres if necessary. Clean up the inside faces, and pre-finish with a lacquer, varnish etc. all inside faces and the lattice frames. Glue the table up, making sure to keep everything square and out of wind, and then clean up the outside faces of the top rails and legs.

10. Rout a 3mm $(\frac{1}{8}'')$ round-over on the outside edge of the legs and top rails. Sand up and finish the outside edges.

Finally, make a hardboard template to fit into the 6mm $(\frac{1}{4}'')$ recess in the top of the table, about 1mm $(\frac{1}{16}'')$ undersize all round, and have a piece of 6mm $(\frac{1}{4}'')$ clear glass cut to it, with polished edges.

Cutting List

Item	No.	Length	Width	Thickness
Top rails and legs	8	420mm $16\frac{1}{2}''$	22mm $\frac{7}{8}''$	22mm $\frac{7}{8}''$
Lower rails	4	420mm $16\frac{1}{2}''$	16mm $\frac{5}{8}''$	16mm $\frac{5}{8}''$
Lattices	12	376mm $14\frac{13}{16}''$	16mm $\frac{5}{8}''$	10mm $\frac{3}{8}''$
Strips	8	360mm $14\frac{3}{16}''$	6mm $\frac{1}{4}''$	4mm $\frac{5}{32}''$

The following router cutters will be needed:

Straight bit	16mm $\frac{5}{8}''$
Straight bit	10mm $\frac{3}{8}''$
Straight bit	6mm $\frac{1}{4}''$
Radius roundover bit	3mm $\frac{1}{8}''$

18. Clocks

Sally James

THIS is a very simple project which shows jig making and the versatility of the small router.

For this exercise I have chosen to make a Morris Minor shaped car clock but this method can be applied to any shape or design. (See Fig. 5).

Machines/tools

Router – mounted upside down in a router table. Small bandsaw or coping saw. Pillar drill or hand drill. Abrasive paper/small files. Self guided 90 degree trimmer/laminate cutter 10mm ($\frac{3}{8}''$) diameter; 6mm ($\frac{1}{4}''$) diameter two fluted router cutter; 10mm ($\frac{3}{8}''$) drill bit.

Materials

2 off 6mm ($\frac{1}{4}''$) Medium Density Fibreboard 170mm ($6\frac{3}{4}''$) × 305mm (12")
1 off 12mm ($\frac{1}{2}''$) Medium Density Fibreboard 305mm (12") × 51mm (2")
1 off Small quartz clock movement
1 off Spray can of primer and cans of coloured paint as desired.

Making the Jig

The jig provides a pattern from which to reproduce many copies of a shape in its exact

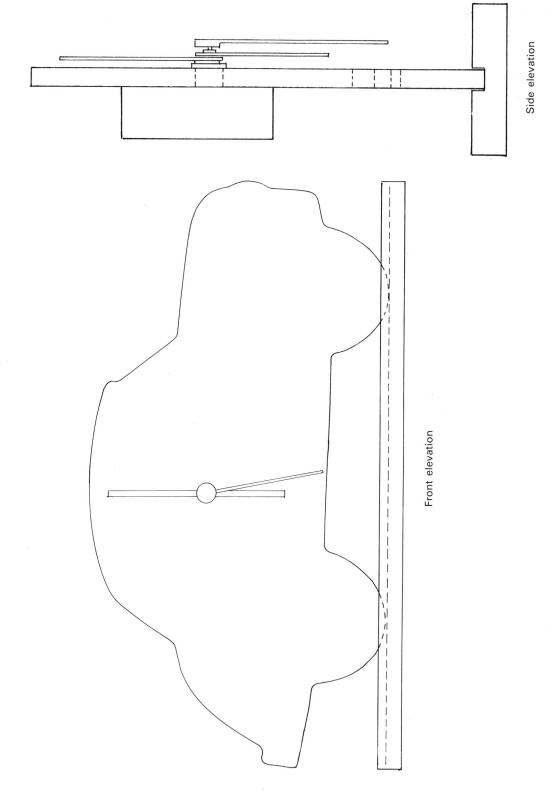

Side elevation

Front elevation

156

form. It is secured to a roughly cut shape and then the bearing on the router cutter follows the profile of the jig and the cutter cuts out the new shape.

Finalise the design on paper, cut it out and place the paper shape on one of the pieces of 6mm ($\frac{1}{4}''$) M.D.F. Draw around it in pencil and using a bandsaw or coping saw cut out the shape, keeping as close to the line as possible.

An important point to note is that sharp inside corners on the jig should be avoided since the router can only cut an inside corner to the radius of the cutter being used – see diagram (Fig. 1).

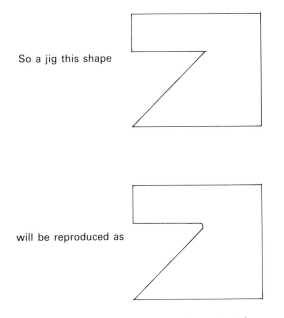

So a jig this shape

will be reproduced as

Fig. 1 The router cutter can only cut inside corners to the size of its own shape

Once the jig has been cut out, smooth off all the rough edges and lumps using abrasive paper or small files if necessary.

When you are satisfied with the shape, hammer two 12mm ($\frac{1}{2}''$) pin tacks through the jig (one in the centre and one towards one end) then snip off part of the length of the pin leaving

approximately 3mm ($\frac{1}{8}''$) protruding through the jig. Now the jig is complete.

Making the clock

Take the other piece of 6mm ($\frac{1}{4}''$) M.D.F., place the jig on it and draw around its edge in pencil. Cut out the shape roughly on the bandsaw or with a coping saw. Place the jig on to the roughly cut shape and tap the pin tacks into it thus securing both parts together. Now the jig is ready to be used.

Safety

Safety is of the utmost importance. A router can be a lethal piece of equipment if mis-used, but when properly used offers an excellent and versatile tool. It is advisable as a matter of safety and comfort to use ear defenders, eye protectors and a mask. When making any adjustments to the cutters always disconnect the power source and use guards wherever possible.

Setting up the router and cutter

Place self-guided bearing cutter in the router, which is fitted into a table. Take the jig and roughly cut shape and use this to set up the height of the router cutter. The bearing must run along the side of the jig, and the cutter needs to be in line with the roughly cut shape – see diagram (Fig. 2).

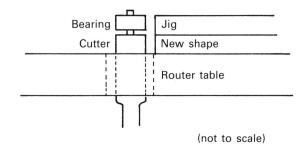

(not to scale)

Fig. 2 The cutter should be set just higher than the thickness of the new shape to ensure a proper cut, not too high. The bearing must run along the jig

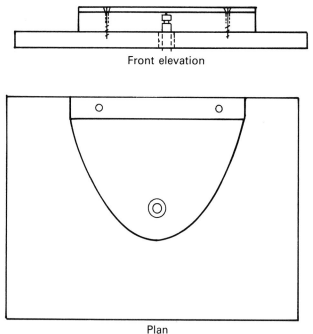

Front elevation

Side elevation

Plan

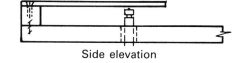

Fig. 3 Use a piece of clean perspex to guard the cutter; an overhang of 50mm (2″) should be sufficient

Set up the guard as in diagram (Fig. 3). The blade turns anti-clockwise so find an easy point to start and then, also in an anti-clockwise motion, trim off the excess M.D.F., making sure that you keep the bearing against the jig as you feed the work round. If you do not turn the work in an anti-clockwise direction the work could easily be taken in the turn of the blade and grabbed from your hold and thus be very dangerous. When the shape has been successfully cut out, pull the jig and clock shape apart. The side of the new shape with the pin holes in becomes the back of the clock. Using abrasive paper remove any burr which may be on the edges of the new shape and then drill a 10mm ($\frac{3}{8}$″) hole in the centre of the shape. (The hole size will depend on the fixing collar of the clock movement.)

Making the clock stand

Cut the 12mm ($\frac{1}{2}$″) M.D.F. to 305mm (12″) × 51mm (2″) and if necessary skim edges with a hand plane. Fit the 6mm ($\frac{1}{4}$″) cutter in the router (still fitted in the table position). The object of the exercise is to cut a central groove approximately 5mm ($\frac{3}{16}$″) deep along its length, using a rule set the height of the cutter. See diagram (Fig. 4) which shows the position of the guards and the best way of carrying out this cut. It may be advisable to make some push sticks to prevent your hands coming into close contact with the cutter. Once the groove has been cut, sand off any burrs to complete the stand.

Spraying the clock and stand

Use a primer spray paint first, this will give a good base on which to use a coloured spray paint and also hide any blemishes in the M.D.F. Apply a couple of coats and lightly sand between each coat. Finally apply a couple of coloured spray paints. Once the paint is completely dry fit the quartz movement and hands. Now the project has been completed and you have a clock and the knowledge to be able to make many more to any design of your choice.

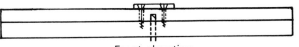

Front elevation

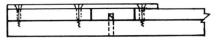

Side elevation

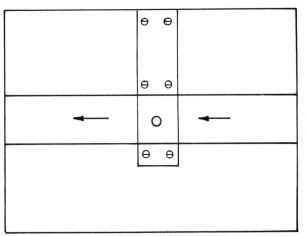

Plan

Fig. 4 Using push sticks pass the work again; use clear perspex to cover the cutter

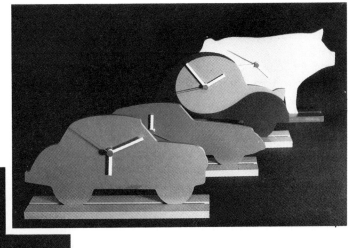

Fig. 5 More designs on the same theme

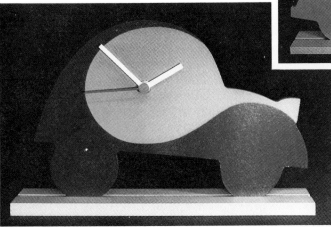

19. An Infill Porch

Les Hurcombe

FROM experience gained while constructing several hundred storm porches, of all types and sizes, the following details and illustrations describe the methods employed to construct one of the more difficult but interesting variations.

Made in hardwood and built up from blocks of contrasting colour, a very strong and attractive porch can be made from using what would normally be regarded as offcuts. A router is essential, but if necessary all the other work could be done by hand.

This is an infill porch to fit a curved brick arch front entrance as built into many thousands of pre-war houses.

The design and setting out of the arched frame is not quite as simple as it may appear. The original timber centring framework constructed for the bricklayers when building the arch is unlikely to have ever been a true symmetrical curve. Even if the frame was orginally built reasonably accurately, after being loaded and unloaded with brickwork, and being dropped on the ground in between, to assume a true curve is risky.

The only way to be sure of a good fit is to hold a sheet or sheets of plywood tight against the brickwork while an assistant draws around the outline with a pencil or felt pen. Some projections such as ornamental tile creases will probably have to be cut off with a disc cutter, and need not be marked. A disc type masonry cutter will be essential if brickwork is to be removed; heavy hammering may cause unacceptable damage to the arch which may already have settlement cracks.

Once you have the ply template with all the essential measurements marked it can be transferred to the workbench.

The bench must be flat and not twisted, any fault will be reproduced as twist or wind in the finished frame. If a large bench or table is not available, place straight timbers onto sawbenches to form a level platform.

Fig. 1 Laying out the ply pattern

The decision about door shape, or double doors, is affected by several important factors.

In a few cases there may be sufficient space for a single door, the main concern here is to allow clearance for the head of the door when opening. The frame may have to be set back to the inside edge of the arch brickwork.

Double doors look right but are not very convenient to use, a pair of 457mm (18″) doors being the absolute minimum, as it is possible to use the one with the latch by itself.

If square tops are acceptable the doors may be made unequal widths, the door in daily use being the larger and the bolted door only opened for dealing with large items such as furniture. The porch shown in the illustrations has round top doors to match the curvature of the arch, the meeting joint in this instance must be central, partly for appearance and also because if the top of one door passes over centre it will not enter the rebate cleanly without excessive clearance.

Outward opening doors should only be used when the inside swing is impossibly restricted. There is a considerable risk of wind damage, even with restrainers, and visitors will not appreciate stepping back to avoid the door.

Sliding doors are only acceptable as a last resort, being very difficult to weatherproof. Water can only be kept out by providing generous drainage channels.

With the example shown the frame and doors follow a common radius.

Lay out the ply pattern, mark the centre line and find the centre of the arc.

Set out the doors to the width required, allow for the 12mm (½″) overlap, if the space is restricted allow a minimum of 100mm (4″) of glass for the sidelights plus the two 50mm (2″) frames. If less, forget the sidelights and make the doors bigger and the frame thicker.

The striking point of the arc must be carefully checked to ensure that there will be sufficient shoulder and head room when entering. Projections on the brickwork will have to be averaged out on the drawing; small amounts can be removed from the frame and some lumps ground off the bricks when fitting.

The doors should be made first so that they

can then be used as a template for marking out the frame.

The door construction follows conventional practice as far as the main cross rails or glazing bars are concerned except that the top rail is omitted. The curved head is added later, made from segments, each joint cut to the radius, glued together with keys plunge-routed into the edge after cleaning up and shaping.

Before the shaping can begin some metalworking is required. Obtain from your local builders' merchant or steel stockholder 1 metre (40″) of steel rod with a diameter to fit the holes in the base of your router. The one end will require flattening sufficiently to take a 6mm ($\frac{1}{4}$″) hole or if welding equipment is accessible fit a washer to the end. Fit this radius rod to a bolt mounted on a bridge fixed over the door stiles. Secure the bridge with screws and mark the ply as this bridge must be detachable to remove and refit the doors. Lock it down tight with two washers and a locknut. This bolt will form the centre of all the cutting of the doors and framework and must be firmly fixed; any flexing or movement will show up in the finish as ripples and steps. All the curves will be cut using this radius arm, including the glazing rebates.

Cut the material for the doors and set out for mortising. For a pair of rebated doors,

Fig. 2 The curved head made up from joined segments

through wedged tenons are not ideal as cutting the meeting joint will expose the wedges and glue line. For the narrow doors the wedges should not be necessary. With good joints and modern adhesive there should be no problem with wide rails fitted, giving a good glue area.

Cut the stiles to length against the template, marking the first top cut with the radius arm.

When the heads of the stiles are cut to the correct bevel and square across, glue, assemble and cramp up the doors in the usual way. Check for square and twist, wipe off surplus glue with a damp cloth.

Fig. 3 The metal radius rod fitted to the router

Lay the doors and sidelights onto the pattern, check that the total width is correct, mark the outlines and then screw plenty of location blocks onto the ply. These blocks must be a good fit to allow for removing and refitting the frames accurately.

The material for the blocks round the curved head will be wider than the stiles to allow for the amount cut away by the router. If 100mm (4″) is used for the stile then 125mm (5″) will be needed for the blocks. Offcuts can be used up here and some waste can be cut away with a bandsaw.

At this stage it will be useful to mark out on the template the radius lines to correspond with block joints. Wide spacing here will require fewer joints and may seem easier and quicker, but wider material will be required and more waste created.

Clean up the doors and clamp onto the pattern, glazing rebate upwards. Fix the centre pin and arm, hold a pencil against the arm and strike the curves of the door head from the stiles.

Place the first block against the angled cut on the top of the stile, take care to cover both inside and outside curves, mark the second joint with a pencil against the radius arm.

Continue round the curve marking each block off the previous cut, make sure of a good fit

Fig. 5 Cleaning up the door

Fig. 6 Checking the shape of the curved head

Fig. 4 All curves are cut using the radius arm

before continuing with the cutting.

A resin glue such as Cascamite should be used, Cascamite has the advantage of being gap filling and also accelerated by heat. With so many joints to be assembled a lot of time can be saved by pre-heating the blocks. Place polythene under the glue lines to protect the pattern.

When the door heads have been assembled and have set, clean off the top surface with plane and sander; take great care when using the plane, small sections may break out of the ends of the blocks. The router base rides over this surface, so keep it flat.

Fix the router onto the radius bar and clamp securely with the cutter edge slightly outside the finish line. You will find that with the heavy cutting involved the hook of the cutter bit will pull the machine slightly inwards. A light finishing cut will give a better finish and more accurate results. For the same reason increase the depth of cut progressively. A block fixed to the router base may help to keep the outer edge up (see Fig. 7).

All the curved cutting on the doors including the glazing rebates should be done without moving the door from the pattern.

Make up the sides of the frame; if glazed side frames, rebated as far as the start of the arch. Then fix down to the template.

The curve of the frame is built up with blocks as before, the difference being that there are two layers with joints overlapped to break joints. The horizontal joint in the layers is arranged to co-incide with the step of the rebate. For this reason the first row of blocks

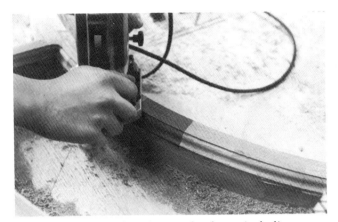

Fig. 8 All the curved cutting on the doors, including the glazing rebates should be done without removing the door from the pattern

will be the same thickness as the doors which form the rebate, the second row, overlapping the joints underneath, forms the door stops (see diagram Fig. 9). The short cross glazing bars shown are inserted as the blocks are built up, rebated before fitting. Any loss of strength from the gluing of end grain is more than compensated for by the overlapping and bonding effect of the brick type jointing.

As the doors do not have the overlapping joints I always insert keys into each joint. Mount the door in the bench vice with the curve upwards. Use a long bit in the router, fit the fence and cut a 12mm ($\frac{1}{2}$") wide mortise 76mm (3") long into the edge of the door across each joint as deep as possible. Plane a hardwood board to a slip fit in the mortises and cut the keys with round ends, glue in and clean off when set. Take care when planing off, the grain on the one end may break out.

When the frame is set, the upper face cleaned up and the edges moulded, do not lift it until

Fig. 7

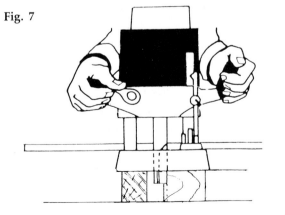

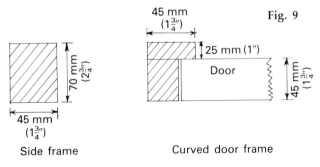

Side frame

Curved door frame

Fig. 9

Fig. 10 Keys set into door joints

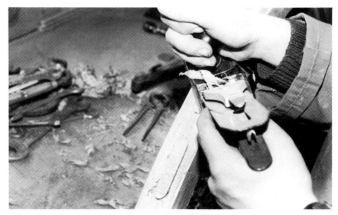

Fig. 11 Planing keys in the door joints

the sill has been fitted. If necessary slide it to the edge of the pattern to work on the ends. Once the sill is fixed two people can invert the frame safely. Turn it over, clean up the face and refix to the pattern.

Continue routing the curves, but before taking the finishing cut off the door rebates lay the finished doors on the frame and mark out onto the frame surface. Fit the router to the radius arm and with the cutter just clearing the surface slide round the curve and test before cutting. Small amounts are best taken off with a rotary sanding drum.

Curved glazing beads are easily made by cutting the curve on a bandsaw, fitting to the frame and then applying the required mould with router held by the radius arm.

I have used this construction for several internal doors in hardwood, extra detail can be applied by using a small diameter bit in the router, 6mm ($\frac{1}{4}''$), and grooving the face to take inserted strings of contrasting colour. Yellow into brown iroko is very attractive and if taken to about 12mm ($\frac{1}{2}''$) deep adds to the strength.

You may find that the letter plate will be more convenient in the fixed door; visitors are less likely to step onto your mail. It may also be possible to fit a basket to the normally fixed door but not the door in constant use.

Finally a tip about the glazing, cutting the curves for the outer frame is easy, lay the 4mm ($\frac{3}{16}''$) glass onto the frame and cut it freehand. Cutting the 6mm ($\frac{1}{4}''$) for the doors is not easy; take the doors to the glazier and let him cut it.

Fig. 12 Small imperfections cleaned up with a rotary sander

Fig. 13 Lay the glass on the frame and cut the curves freehand

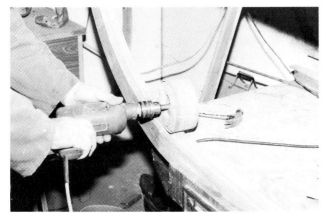

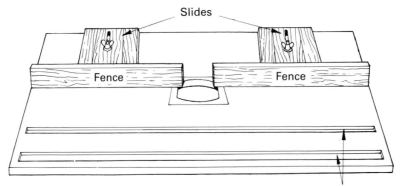

Slides

Fence   Fence

Slots for tee square

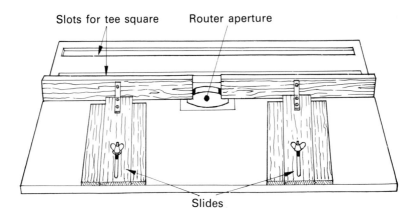

Slots for tee square   Router aperture

Slides

20. Routing Table

V.J. Taylor

THERE must be many woodworkers who, like me, have one of the Black & Decker's folding "Workmate" benches. And, also like me, they have only restricted space to work in so that any equipment which can be hung on the wall or stacked away flat when not in use is a godsend. I made up this router table, which can be clamped into a Workmate and is less than 60mm (2⅜″) deep, and have found it ideal for use with an Elu router.

The table is 915mm × 610mm (36″ × 24″), and is made from some 11mm ($\frac{7}{16}$″) chipboard I had by me; however, with the benefit of hindsight, I think the same thickness in M.D.F (medium

density fibreboard) would be much better for the job.

First of all, make sure that the table is perfectly rectangular and then mark out some datum lines on what will be the underside. These are shown in Fig. 1, and as you can see, comprise the two diagonals and the two lines which bisect the sides – if the table is truly rectangular they should all meet in the same central point.

Now choose any cutter with a sharp point and insert it into your router; position the router as shown in plan view in Fig. 1, and plunge the bit almost to touch the table surface.

166

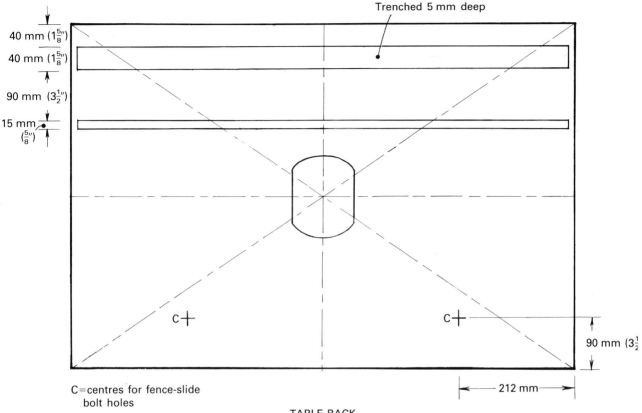

Trenched 5 mm deep

40 mm $(1\frac{5}{8}'')$

40 mm $(1\frac{5}{8}'')$

90 mm $(3\frac{1}{2}'')$

15 mm $(\frac{5}{8}'')$

90 mm $(3\frac{1}{2}$

212 mm

C=centres for fence-slide bolt holes

TABLE-BACK

Fig. 1 Plan view of table: dotted datum lines are on the underside

Move it around until it is precisely over the central point you have marked. Then pencil round the outline of the router base, and cut it out so that the router base will fit snugly into the aperture.

The white rectangular panel on the upper (working) surface of the table is optional. I inserted it because I am a great believer in marking out from the actual job rather than setting it out theoretically, and this often involves drawing pencil lines to mark where the fences should be fixed. If the pencil lines are not drawn heavily, you can erase them easily. The panel is simply a piece of white plastic laminate which is stuck down, and the recess can be easily routed out using the adjustable side fence on the router's extension

rods, locating the fence to run against the table sides. The size is not significant – as a guide, mine is 178mm × 147mm (7″ × 5¾″).

To complete the routing on the working surface you will need to rout out two channels for a small tee-square (described later) to run in. The purpose of this tee-square is to keep the work square to the fence when cutting tenons. Again, the sizes and positions of these channels are not critical and you can make them to suit your own requirements; for guidance, I have given the dimensions of mine in Fig. 1. The small, inner channel accommodates the small block on the tee-square and helps it to remain perfectly at right-angles in use.

Next we come to the method of mounting

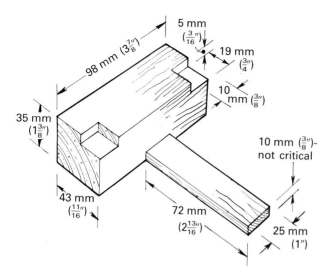

Fig. 2 Diagram of an end cramping block

critical. The length must be 98mm ($3\frac{7}{8}''$) so that the blocks can be inserted into the vice jaws and cramped up tightly; the distance strips must protrude 72mm ($2\frac{13}{15}''$) exactly, as they butt against the spring-loaded columns of the router; and the recesses for housing the ends of the extension rods must be 19mm ×10mm × 5mm ($\frac{3}{4}'' \times \frac{3}{8}'' \times \frac{3}{16}''$) deep.

To set up the assembly, insert the extension rods into their housings on the router in the usual way and cramp up one of the blocks in the Workmate vice jaws. Lay the ends of the extension rods into their recesses on this block and then do the same with the block at the other end of the extension rods. You will find that the distance strips will ensure that the router is held centrally, and the assembly is shown in Fig. 3. At this point, I should mention that if you can find two bolts to replace the locking screws for the extension rods and use them to clamp the router on to the rods, it is a good idea, but not essential.

Returning now to the table, set up the router, extension rods, and blocks in their working position in the Workmate; you will notice that although the router cannot move laterally, it is free to move upwards. To prevent this happening you need to do two things. First, on the underside of the table top, mark round the outline of the Workmate vice jaws; then glue and pin 25mm × 6mm ($1'' \times \frac{1}{4}''$) wood strips

the router. The widest gap to which the vice jaws on the Workmate will open is slightly over 102mm (4"); you will find that if you turn the router upside-down you can lift its base up through this gap and it will, in fact, rest on the vice jaws. However, it is advisable to remove the locking screws which normally clamp the extension rods as they are not needed and can jam against the vice jaws.

The next step is to make up a pair of end cramping blocks (one left- and one right-hand) to the sizes shown in Fig. 2; here, the sizes are

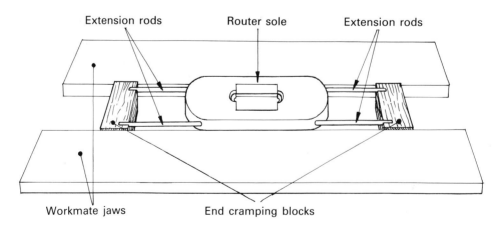

Fig. 3 The inverted router, extension rods, and end cramping blocks in the Workmate vice jaws

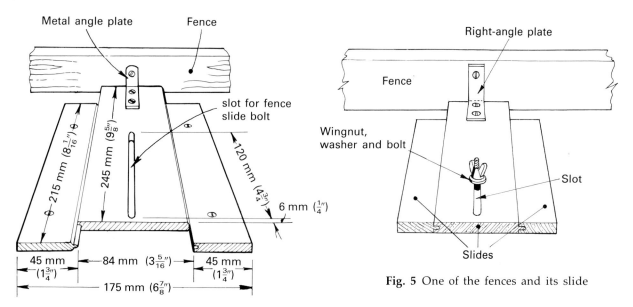

Fig. 4 A fence and adjustable slide. (Two required)

Fig. 5 One of the fences and its slide

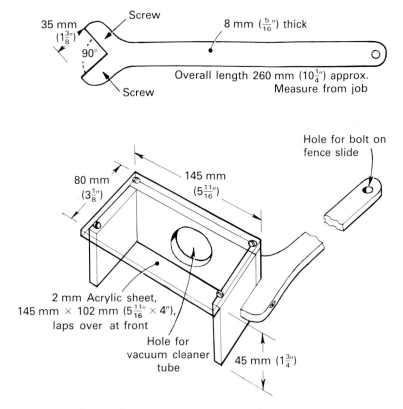

Fig. 6 Above, shape and sizes of the rear guard-arm; below, details of the guard-box

around the outline. This means that when you put the table top on to the Workmate, the strips will automatically locate it in the correct position. Second, fix a small thumb-cramp at each end of the table to cramp it down on to the Workmate so that everything is held down firmly.

Now for the adjustable fences. I have used an idea which I have employed before as it gives a smooth and accurate method of adjustment. To make the two adjustable slides you will need a length of ordinary 90mm ($3\frac{1}{2}''$) wide tongued-and-grooved board about 915mm (36") long and 10mm ($\frac{3}{8}''$) thick. I have shown the dimensions in Fig. 4. Cut off two 245mm ($9\frac{5}{8}''$) lengths and sand them. Each piece has a slot cut down its centre which accepts a 50mm × 5mm ($2'' \times \frac{3}{16}''$) bolt, with its accompanying washer and wing-nut.

A fence is attached to the end of each of these slides – the size of the fence is not critical – mine are 425mm × 45mm × 19mm ($16\frac{3}{4}'' \times 1\frac{3}{4}'' \times \frac{3}{4}''$). As it happened I had some right-angled repair plates by me and, once they had been drilled for screws and hacksawn to size, I screwed one to each slide and fence as shown, and glued the joint for good measure. However,

the fixing could just as well be made with wooden blocks, glued and screwed in place.

To make the side pieces in which the slides run, cut the remaining piece of t & g board in half, lengthwise, and then cut across each piece at its middle so that you have four pieces of the same length. Screw each piece into position exactly at right-angles to the edge of the table with the tongue matched to the groove, so that the slide moves sweetly. A little candle grease rubbed along the tongues will help. Fig. 5 shows you a finished slide.

The guard at the back of the fences is simply a three-sided box with the open side facing towards the router cutter; the top is a piece of 2mm ($\frac{1}{16}''$) acrylic sheet screwed down. This allows you to see any build-up of shavings, dust etc, which is an advantage, but you could use a piece of hardboard instead. In the rear side of the guard-box a hole is cut into which you can push the nozzle of a vacuum-cleaner tube. As these are usually tapered, a push-fit is all that is needed, this will get rid of most of the shavings. Measurements are given in Fig. 6, together with details of the arm, which swivels on one of the bolts holding down a slide. Figs. 7 and 8 show the general arrangement with

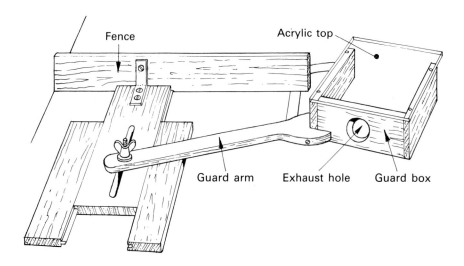

Fig. 7 The rear-guard, from the back of the table

170

the guard-box in close-up.

The tee-square is quite straightforward to make; details are given in Fig. 9 and again, you can adapt them to suit your own requirements.

Fig. 10a illustrates how the holding-down device is assembled; Fig. 10b gives the dimensions of the component pieces. The device also acts as an effective guard for the router cutter while working. The moulding which holds the work down is a short piece of right-angled moulding 75mm (3") long, each arm being 40mm (1⅝") wide; this is readily obtainable at any DIY store.

The moulding can be moved up or down against the upstand by means of the bolts through the slots, to suit the size of work being done. The base is cramped to the table in any convenient position; by moving the upstand backwards, even the smallest moulding can be held between the end of the base and the fence

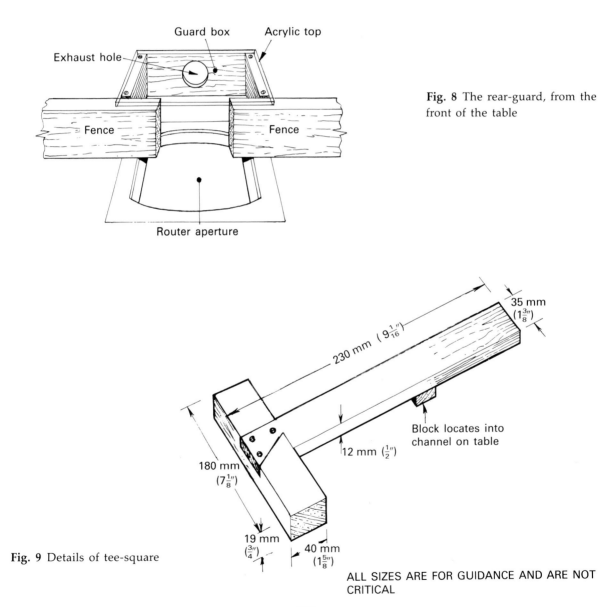

Fig. 8 The rear-guard, from the front of the table

Fig. 9 Details of tee-square

ALL SIZES ARE FOR GUIDANCE AND ARE NOT CRITICAL

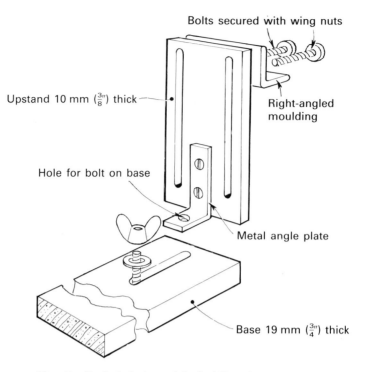

Fig. 10a Exploded view of the holding-down accessory

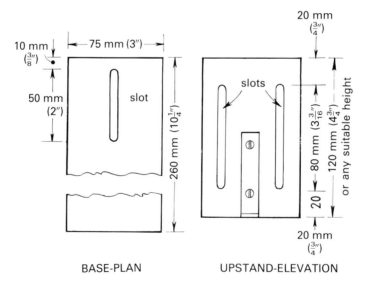

BASE-PLAN   UPSTAND-ELEVATION

Fig. 10b Plan and elevation

while being routed. The moulding can also be lowered to hold the work down so that you can work in perfect safety.

Although the table was designed primarily for use with a Workmate, it could easily be adapted to become a free-standing router table in its own right. You would need to fit a conventional frame and legs; each end cramping block would need a hole drilled through it so that it could be bolted to the underside of the table when fitting in the router and its extension rods as shown in Fig. 3. These bolts could be tightened by means of wing nuts – it would also be advisable to clamp the router in the centre of the extension rods by means of its clamping screws. These small changes are all that would be needed to complete the modification.

Publications of related interest

from

STOBART DAVIES LTD

World Woods in Colour *William Lincoln*—275 commercial world timbers in full colour, describing general characteristics, properties and uses table. 300 pages.

Wood Machining *Nigel Voisey*—A fresh approach to the most important area of workshop practice—safety. Approx. 160pp photographs and line drawings.

Spindle Moulder Handbook *Eric Stephenson*—Covers all aspects of this essential woodworking machine from spindle speeds to grinding and profiling. 200 pages—430 photos and line drawings.

Marketing & Promotion for Crafts *Betty Norbury*—Masses of good, sound advice for sales and marketing for all makers and designers of wood and other craftwork. 126pp.

Fundamentals of Figure Carving *Ian Norbury*—A highly visual study, illustrated with over 300 superb drawings and photographs of carving the human figure in wood. 160pp.

Projects for Creative Woodcarving *Ian Norbury*—Over 50 projects to inspire the woodcarver. Beautifully illustrated.

The Village Carpenter *Walter Rose*—A new reprint of this classic 1930's work. 192pp.

What Wood is that? *Herbert Edlin*—A manual of wood identification. Contains 40 actual wood veneer samples. 160pp illustrated.

The Complete Manual of Wood Finishing *Frederick Oughton*—An encyclopædic work on the traditional craft of wood finishing. 288pp illustrated. Highly detailed and extensive.

The Complete Manual of Wood Veneering *William Lincoln*—Extensive coverage of all the techniques used in furniture and craftwork. 400 pages. Fully illustrated.

Techniques of Creative Woodcarving *Ian Norbury*—A complete work with emphasis on the practical side of figure carving. 160pp, 200 illustrations.

A Glossary of Wood *Thomas Corkhill*—10,000 terms defined in this unique book. Includes 1,000 line diagrams and drawings. 672pp.

Beyond Basic Turning *Jack Cox*—This wood turning book covers off-centre, coopered, laminated and segmented work. Very detailed with over 300 illustrations and explicit instructions to help produce fine turned work. 256pp.

Artistic Woodturning *Dale L. Nish*—Step by step instructions with more than 700 photographs including 39 in full colour. 264pp.

Creative Woodturning *Dale L. Nish*—Step by step instructions for the woodturner. 630 photographs. 256pp., 8 in colour.

Techniques of Spiral Work *Stuart Mortimer*—A complete treatise of making all types of twist work by hand and on the lathe. 192pp.

The Construction of Period Country Furniture *V. J. Taylor*—28 designs of period furniture to make. Includes complete constructional details and plans. 192pp. Illustrated.

Art & Craft of Making Children's Furniture *Chris Simpson*—Plenty of exciting and original designs for the woodworker to make. Colour throughout. 176pp.

The Conversion & Seasoning of Wood *Wm. H. Brown*—A guide to principles and practice covering all aspects of timber conversion from the log and dealing with proven methods of seasoning. 222 pages illustrated.

Machine Woodworking Technology for Hand Woodworkers *F. E. Sherlock*—Covers virtually all the machines and associated technology that the hand woodworker is likely to encounter. 214 pages, illustrated throughout.

The Marquetry Manual *Wm. A. Lincoln*—This state-of-the-art publication incorporates all the traditional ideas and practices for marquetarians as well as all the current thinking, and a selection of some of the greatest marquetry pictures. 272 pages, 400 illustrations.

Relief Woodcarving and Lettering *Ian Norbury*—Caters for all levels of ability from beginners onwards, exploring the fields of low and high relief carving through a series of graded projects. 157 pages, fully illustrated.

Modern Practical Joinery *George Ellis*—This vast coverage of internal joinery includes windows, doors, stairs, handrails, mouldings, shopfitting and showcase work, all clearly detailed and illustrated with hundreds of line drawings. Nearly 500 pages and 27 chapters.

Mouldings and Turned Woodwork of the 16th, 17th & 18th Centuries *T. Small & C. Woodbridge* This large format book presents full size details and sections of staircases, doors, panelling, skirtings, windows, together with architectural turnings and many other specific applications of mouldings.

Book of Boxes *Andrew Crawford*—A complete practical guide to box making and box design. Clear step-by-step drawings and photographs in full colour throughout. 144pp.

Further information from:

STOBART DAVIES LTD.
Specialist Publishers & Booksellers
PRIORY HOUSE, 2 PRIORY STREET, HERTFORD SG14 1RN
(Tel: 01992 501518)